ANIMAL CHAMPIONS

Written by RONALD ROOD

Line drawings by H.B. VESTAL

Collins · Glasgow and London

Introduction

Suppose you are out for an afternoon walk. Perhaps you are strolling through an old pasture, or maybe you are on a tour of the city park. No matter where you are, there are animals about you. A frog jumps into a pool. Squirrels search for nuts and seeds. You slap at a mosquito.

Suddenly there is the sound of wings in the air. A bird flaps away from an old tree above your head. It is a hawk – the largest bird you have ever seen.

This starts you thinking. Are there any birds larger than that hawk? What about other creatures – the whale and the elephant? Which of them is larger? And how about the great *Brontosaurus*? Was this dinosaur the largest animal of them all?

Then there are other questions. Which is the strongest animal? The swiftest? Which animal lives the longest?

These are just a few thoughts that may come to mind as you watch the living things around you. The same questions have arisen in my mind, too. And so this book has come into being. It explores the world of the pasture, the city park, the forest and the ocean. Here you will find the fastest flyer, the greatest jumper, the deepest diver.

Many of these animals can be found only in far-off places of the earth. Some of them, however, may be right there beside you. This book will help point them out, no matter where they are. It tells of the fascinating creatures that could easily win medals, if nature gave out prizes. It is the story of the Animal Champions.

First published in this edition 1973
Published by William Collins Sons and Company Limited, Glasgow and London
© 1969 by Grosset and Dunlap Inc. All rights reserved under International and
Pan-American Copyright Conventions.
© 1973 additional text and photographs William Collins Sons and Company Limited
Printed in Great Britain
ISBN 0 00 106190 9

Contents

Acknowledgement

The author and publisher gratefully
acknowledge their indebtedness to

WALTER C. FABELL

for the idea for this book, and for
research and other work which helped
in its creation.

A buzzard captures a mouse.

1 From towering giants to microscopic specks

Where an animal lives dictates its size

Animals come in all shapes and sizes. There are tall slender giraffes, long sleek snakes, quick little mice, slow tortoises and mighty elephants. Sometimes it is hard to decide just why an animal may be the way it is. But scientists can usually find a reason.

The reason is often simply that our world has a great many places in which to live. Each one of them might make a home for some animal if that animal could fit exactly into that spot.

Take a good look at the next animal you see. It may be a feathered animal – a bird. And if your bird is a buzzard or owl, you may see how its large size allows it to pick up a mouse or some other animal and carry it away with powerful wings. A large goose or swan can float on water and reach to the bottom of the pond with its long neck. If you watch a heron or crane, you can see how its tall body and long legs help it wade in swamps and marshes.

Even the small size of other birds helps them fit into their place in life. If your bird is a sparrow, you can watch it pick up small insects or peck the seeds from plants. And if you happen to see a humming-bird, you can watch it quickly insert its slender beak into a flower to reach a drop of sweet nectar at the blossom's base. If the tiny humming-bird tried to rest on the flower, it would crush it, but its fast-beating wings let it hover in mid-air while it feeds.

If your animal is a mouse, think how tiny it really is. Its little front feet are hardly bigger than one of the letters on this page. Yet such a small creature is perfectly suited for life among the grass roots. A rabbit is much larger than a mouse, and is good at hopping along forest paths and feeding on low bushes or nibbling clover.

If you could watch an elephant in the jungle, you would see how its huge size is just right for its life, too. With its long trunk it can reach up and pull down leafy branches for food. It even pushes small trees to earth so that it can feed on their topmost leaves. Great size also protects the elephant, for there are few enemies large enough to attack it.

Of course there are many other ways in which animals differ from each other besides size and shape. But whether an animal has big feet, funny ears, or merely looks as if it should go on a diet, it is probably because it is best suited for its own special life.

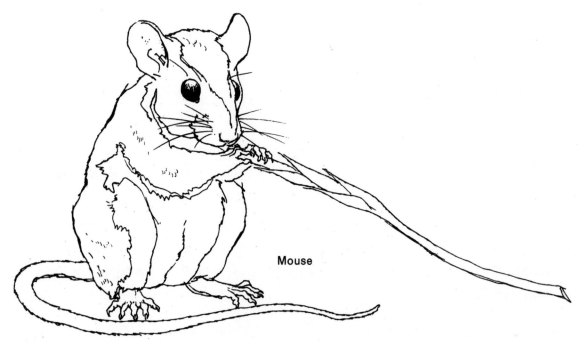

Mouse

Largest of living land animals, an African elephant spreads his great ears for the slightest sound. He can hear the rustle of a mouse in the leaves at his feet.

Elephants are the largest living land animals

The African elephant is the largest land animal known today. Bulls, or male elephants, are somewhat larger than the females, or cows. An Indian bull elephant may be as much as 3 metres (10 feet) high at the shoulder, and a large African bull elephant may reach 3·35 metres (11 feet) in height. Such a gigantic creature may weigh nearly 7 tonnes.

Jumbo, the famous circus animal, was an African bull elephant. He stood 3·50 metres (11 feet 6 inches) at the shoulder. P. T. Barnum, the famous showman who exhibited Jumbo and gave people rides on his back, probably never knew the great animal's exact weight. However, Jumbo must have weighed between 6 and 7 tonnes. Jumbo's skeleton is at the American Museum of Natural History in New York City.

The giraffe is the tallest animal

Even if you were sitting on Jumbo's back, it would still be necessary to look up to a good-sized giraffe. It may be as much as 4·87 metres (16 feet) tall.

Most of a giraffe's height is made up of its slender legs and long neck. These enable it to reach up into trees for tender leaves and twigs which it eats with its hairy lips and very long tongue. It is, indeed, the tallest animal that walks the earth today.

The great whale is the largest animal known

If you were an explorer, you could probably search every continent without finding any creature larger than an elephant or taller than a giraffe. To find the largest animal of all you would have to search in the mysterious depths of the sea.

In your search you might come across all kinds of great creatures. The sea is so large that scientists do not know exactly what kinds of animals it contains. There are great squids more than 15 metres (50 feet) long and huge sharks which weigh many tonnes. There are even jellyfish as big as bathtubs.

The largest of all, however, are not squids or sharks or jellyfish. They are so huge that all other known creatures on the earth or in the sea look tiny by comparison. These are the great whales. Although they are shaped like fish, whales are really not fish at all. Fish are cold-blooded, but whales have warm bodies and feed their young with milk, as do dogs, cats, people and even tiny mice. Such animals are known as mammals.

These sea mammals come in many sizes. The smaller ones are known as dolphins, or porpoises, and may be only 1·83 or 2·44 metres (6 or 8 feet) long. You have probably seen them on television or in a marine aquarium. There are middle-sized whales 6·09 or 9·14 metres (20 or 30 feet) long. But the greatest of them all is the blue whale. This is truly a giant of the sea. The largest blue whale known – over 33·52 metres (110 feet) long, is the largest animal known to science.

Able to look through a first floor window, the giraffe can find its food in the treetops.

The large blue whale: What it looks like and how it lives

If you were out in a boat and a blue whale suddenly came to the surface, you would hardly be able to believe your eyes. Whales have been known to surface next to steamships. Looking like great grey rocks rising out of the water, they have been heard emitting loud sounds like sighs as they let out their breath. Then, taking a new breath through the blowhole, they sink out of sight.

Just how large would a great blue whale be if you could bring it on land? Suppose you put that 33·52 metre (110 foot) specimen on a lawn tennis court with its nose resting on one baseline. At the other end its tail would extend beyond the limits of the court for another 9·75 metres (32 feet). And scientists believe that if you could put such a huge creature on scales, it would weigh as much as 173 tonnes (170 tons). This is about the same as the combined weight of 170 motor cars!

For all its bulk, the huge whale feeds on tiny sea creatures which look rather like little floating lobsters. These creatures are krill and may be only an inch or two long. The whale strains them from sea water by means of its baleen, a special strainer in its huge mouth.

Dinosaur

Blue Whale

The dinosaur would have lost the contest, if the blue whale had been there

There were no whales in the days of the dinosaurs. In fact, mammals had not developed very far in those prehistoric times. But even the great Brontosaurus, one of the largest dinosaurs, was scarcely a third as big as a good-sized blue whale. It may have reached 21·33 metres (70 feet) from nose to tail, but much of its length was made up of the long slender neck and tail. Like many of the other large dinosaurs, it floated its huge bulk in water much of the time.

14

It is hard to tell if this ostrich is looking at her own chicks or not. The great eggs, weighing as much as 1·36 kilograms (3 pounds) each, may be laid by several females in a single nest.

The giant among birds

The largest bird today cannot fly. This is the ostrich of the African desert. A full-grown male ostrich may weigh over 136 kilograms (300 pounds) and may be almost 2·74 metres (9 feet) tall. Its legs may be 1·22 metres (4 feet) long and it is strong enough to carry a man on its back. In Africa you can go for an ostrich ride just as you can take a pony ride here. A single ostrich egg may contain as much food as a dozen hens' eggs.

One of the rarest birds of North America is the California condor, with a wing-span of more than 2·5 metres (8 feet).

For the bird with the greatest wing-span, look seaward

Probably the greatest wing-span belongs to a bird of the sea. The wandering albatross is a bird with a body about the size of a goose, but with wings which allow it to soar over the ocean for hours without effort. Many albatrosses have a wing-span of about 3 metres (10 feet). One of these birds had a span of nearly 3·65 metres (12 feet). Its wings measured 3·29 metres (11 feet 10 inches) from tip to tip. The Andean condor of South America has a wing-span almost as great. Its wings have been known to spread 3 metres (10 feet).

The reptile giant

The greatest snakes are the Asiatic pythons and the anaconda of South America. Often you hear stories of impressive lengths of these reptiles, but many of them are based on somebody's guess. The longest snake to be measured accurately was an anaconda – over 11 metres (37 feet) long.

Crocodiles often appear to be larger than they are because water magnifies them. Besides, they are so fearsome that they appear to be giants. Actually, a specimen more than 4 metres (15 feet) long is unusual today. One of the largest ones measured had a length of over 6·09 metres (20 feet).

There are many stories about huge sea turtles, too. Even a specimen measuring 60 centimetres (2 feet) long would seem large if you suddenly came across it while you were swimming. The leatherback turtle of the Pacific Ocean is actually the largest of the turtles. Its shell may be 152 centimetres (5 feet) long. Such a great creature may weigh more than 901 kilograms (1,900 pounds).

The largest fish

It would be hard to decide which fish was largest of all. In the first place, many fish grow slowly all through life. Then, too, not all kinds of fish will take a hook, so perhaps they have never been caught and weighed.

A blue marlin weighing 342 kilograms (756 pounds) was caught near Puerto Rico. A swordfish caught near Chile weighed 534 kilograms (1,182 pounds), and a bluefin tuna caught off the Nova Scotia coast weighed 443 kilograms (977 pounds). Even larger than these were a black marlin caught near Peru weighing 706 kilograms (1,560 pounds) and a 1,369 kilogram (2,664 pound) white shark near Australia in 1959.

The greatest fish of them all, however, is hardly likely to be caught on a line. This is the whale shark, a peaceful and slow creature in spite of its size. A large whale shark may be 15·24 metres (50 feet) long. Scientists think that it may weigh more than 40 tonnes!

The giant among insects

Honours for weight would probably go to the Goliath beetle of Africa. It is almost as big as a banana, with a wing-span of 20 centimetres (8 inches). Wings of even greater spread, however, are found on many moths. The Atlas moth of the tropics may have a wing-span of 30 centimetres (12 inches) or more.

The longest insects are known as the walking sticks. They live in the tropics and may be 30 centimetres (1 foot) or more long.

The tiniest insect

The smallest insect of all may not have been discovered. Scientists feel there are many insects in this world that are still unknown. A small insect, of course, could easily be overlooked. Even so, few could be much smaller than a tiny wasp known as the fairy-fly. Two of these little creatures could fit on the full stop at the end of this sentence. It would take a hundred of them, placed end to end, to cover $2\frac{1}{2}$ centimetres (an inch). To find them you would have to look inside the eggs of other insects.

The smallest mammal

Many people think that a mouse must be the smallest of the mammals. There is a little brown animal, however, that is much smaller. This is a pygmy shrew, found in southern Europe, a creature so small that its entire body may be only 38 millimetres ($1\frac{1}{2}$ inches) long. Its newborn babies are so tiny that it would take fifty of them to weigh 0·02 kilograms (1 ounce).

The smallest bird

Even the pygmy shrew is bigger than the smallest of humming-birds. While the humming-bird may be as long as the shrew, nearly half its length is made up of its slender bill. The smallest humming-birds of all may have a body only a little longer than a honeybee – barely $2\frac{1}{2}$ centimetres (1 inch).

With eggs the size of peas and a nest no larger than a golf ball, the humming-bird is a midget among birds.

The smallest animal of all is not visible to the naked eye

You would need a fine microscope to see the world's smallest animals. Even then, you would hardly recognise them as animals, for they have no eyes or legs or other familiar parts. For a mouth they may have a little scoop, or they may merely surround food slowly from every direction until it is within their bodies.

These animals are known as protozoans. A few types of protozoans, including the amoeba, are large enough to be seen with the naked eye in good light. The smallest protozoans, however, are unbelievably small. Fifty of them, side by side, would just reach across the width of a human hair.

2 Each has its own pace

For their own protection, some animals are much faster than others

As you look at a tortoise plodding along, you may wonder why it is so slow when a rabbit is so fast.

The answer may be there in front of you. When a fox discovers a rabbit, the rabbit must run for its life. Its protection is in its long legs and ability to twist and dodge while running. The tortoise, of course, just hides in its shell until danger is over. Then it goes poking along as if nothing has happened.

Each animal has its own way of protecting itself. It also has its own way of earning a living. If a lion were as slow as a tortoise, it could never catch any animals. So an animal may be speedy to escape from danger, or it may be able to run fast in order to catch its food.

Although frogs, small mammals and birds make up its main diet, a skunk will eat almost anything it finds. It therefore does not need to chase its food. And because of its scent gun, it does not need to run away from enemies. Just as you might suspect, a skunk is a slow-moving, peaceful little animal.

The race between the tortoise and the hare could be a tie

Perhaps you know the old story of the contest between the tortoise and a hare. The hare, which is an animal similar to a rabbit, lost the race because it stopped to sleep along the way.

This might happen today, too. However, it might happen the other way as well. Hares can run as fast as 48 kilometres (30 miles) an hour, but both tortoises and hares may go to sleep during the day. Then, too, a hare often runs in a big circle without getting very far from home. A tortoise might go in a straight line for a while – and then hide beneath an old log for a week. So the race might not get anywhere at all.

The snail's pace

People often say that things are travelling at a snail's pace when they are going very slowly. But just how slowly does a snail travel? This depends upon the snail, and it also depends on the weather. Snails travel by first spreading down a layer of slimy material, or mucus, and then gliding along on it. When the weather is too cold or too dry, the snail does not travel at all. It may close itself up in its shell for days or even weeks. A slug, a kind of a snail without a shell, can travel just about 30 centimetres (1 foot) per minute. At this rate, if it travelled night and day, it would have taken nearly four days to go 1·6 kilometres (1 mile)!

Slow-motion champion, the wood snail would take half a day to travel the length of a football field – even under the best of conditions.

The three-toed sloth hangs in a tree through rain and sunshine. Its hair even grows the wrong way so that it can shed water while the sloth hangs upside down.

The slowest animal could be mistaken for a sleep walker

There are a great many animals that never seem to go anywhere at all. Yet they get along well just the same. Oysters or coral, for example, start out as tiny floating animals. They may drift for many kilometres in ocean currents. Finally they settle down, develop a hard outer covering, and stay in one place for the rest of their lives. Flowing ocean water brings food to them in the form of tiny plants and animals.

Many other sea animals stay in one place. Sea lilies and sea anemones look more like plants than animals. Sponges are really animals, too, but they also depend on the ocean to supply their food.

Perhaps the slowest mammal is the three-toed sloth. Living in the American tropics, this animal often hangs upside-down from a limb. It climbs so slowly that it seems to be in a dream. If you saw one sleeping in a tree, you might wonder what it was, for the thick fur on its 4·5 kilogram (10 pound) body makes it look like a bird's nest, or a bunch of last year's leaves. Baby sloths can climb about as fast as human babies can move. With age they get slower and sleepier. A sloth usually does not go far. Tired out by all its activity, it soon falls fast asleep.

22

Beautiful but poisonous, the sea anemone spreads its tentacles like an underwater flower, waiting for a fish to brush against its deadly tentacles.

The motionless insect

Often when something never moves we say it stays there like a bump on a log. Not only do some insects not move, but they even look like tiny bumps on a twig or log. These are the strange creatures known as scale insects.

Scale insects may run over twigs when they are young, but when they become adults they grow a shell, like a tiny turtle's. Protected by this shell, they remain in one place, sucking the sap from the plant with their sharp beaks.

Perhaps you have seen scale insects without realising it. Sometimes they are on grapefruits, oranges or other fruits. They are often flat and oval in shape, and look like little flecks of brown paint on fruit or on a twig or branch.

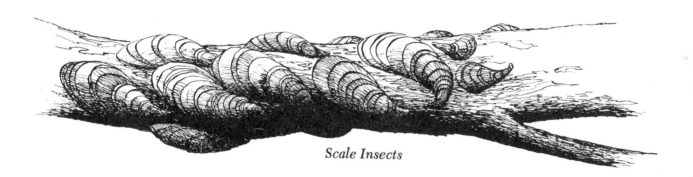

Scale Insects

The fastest insect

As with other creatures, it is difficult to measure the speed of insects. They may dart through the air at high speed, but for only a short distance. One of the fastest insects known is the botfly. This is a creature that lays its eggs on the hair of horses, so it must be able to keep up with them if they run away. Botflies have been known to reach 80 kilometres (50 miles) an hour.

Another speed king is the dragonfly. Looking like a little aeroplane with four wings sticking out at the sides, it can also reach 80 kilometres (50 miles) an hour.

Like winged bullets, the dragonflies dart after mosquitoes and other insects in the air above a pond or meadow.

Four cheetahs, some of the swiftest of all runners, begin the hunt in Africa's Kruger National Park.

The race of the mammals

A large dog could probably run for a short distance alongside a car going at 32 kilometres (20 miles) an hour. If the dog happened to be a greyhound it could race along at about 48 kilometres (30 miles) an hour. A fine race-horse could keep up with a car travelling at 64 kilometres (40 miles) an hour, although it would soon slow down. A deer can travel at about the same speed as a horse. The pronghorn of western North America is even faster. It can travel at 96 kilometres (60 miles) an hour, a mile a minute. Although wolves are not much faster than dogs, they sometimes catch the pronghorn by taking turns at chasing it until it is tired.

African antelopes, black bucks and gazelles can also travel at about 80 kilometres (50 miles) an hour for short distances. Few animals can catch them in a straight race. There is one other creature which can run as fast. This is the cheetah of Africa and India.

The cheetah is often called the hunting leopard. Spotted like a leopard, it is a long-legged member of the cat family, with a body about 1·21 metres (4 feet) long and a long tail. Like a dog, it can be easily tamed and has been used in hunting for thousands of years. It can make short bursts of speed up to 96 kilometres (60 miles) an hour. Although higher speeds have been claimed, these are probably exaggerated.

The speed at which birds fly

When we say fast as a bird, just how fast do we mean? There are so many birds that this can be a great variety of speeds. Even the same bird will fly faster at some times than at others. In a stiff wind, a bird will have to fly hard just to stay in one place over the ground. If it turns and goes the other way, the wind whisks it away in a moment. So ground speed and air speed may be quite different.

Birds usually fly faster when there is some reason for speed. For example, a hawk and the bird it is chasing may both fly faster than when each is alone. A swallow can dart after an insect at a speed twice as fast as it normally flies.

Many of our familiar birds fly at 32 to 48 kilometres (20 to 30 miles) an hour. The common starling may reach 80 kilometres (50 miles) an hour when it is chased. Humming-birds have been known to dart along at 112 kilometres (70 miles) an hour. The golden eagle can fly at 128 kilometres (80 miles) an hour, while the spine-tailed swift, generally regarded as the fastest-moving of all creatures, travels at over 160 kilometres (100 miles) an hour.

Some birds run faster than they can fly

The road runner of the southwestern United States is a funny-looking bird. Although its long legs, neck and tail make it look almost like a little crane, it is a member of the cuckoo family. There is nothing funny about its speed, however. It can fly, but it usually runs over the ground. When it chases lizards and desert snakes, it may reach 32 kilometres (20 miles) an hour. This may be faster than it can fly, especially if it has to fly into the wind.

The Australian emu is a large bird which looks rather like the ostrich of Africa. It can run as fast as 48 kilometres (30 miles) an hour. But the ostrich is even faster. It has been known to run at almost 80 kilometres (50 miles) an hour. Neither of these birds has wings large enough to enable it to fly.

Lizard

Road Runner

The fastest birds

Top honours in bird speeds go to the swift and the peregrine falcon. You may have seen chimney swifts flying overhead in summer. A chimney swift is sometimes called a cigar with wings, for it is a short, dark, slender bird with long, pointed wings and almost no tail. Some Asiatic swifts have been known to reach 144 kilometres (90 miles) an hour.

The peregrine falcon is sometimes known as the duck hawk. This rare bird nests on cliffs near water. Peregrine falcons have also been known to nest on the ledges of tall buildings.

Like the swift, the peregrine falcon has been known to fly at 144 kilometres (90 miles) an hour. It can move even faster in a dive. Hurtling down from the sky, the grey bullet has been known to reach 289 kilometres (180 miles) an hour.

29

Tops among flyers, falcons can dive at 4.82 kilometres (3 miles) a minute.

The speed at which fish swim

If you ever caught a bass or trout, you probably felt that the fish was tearing through the water at a great speed. It may surprise you to know that it was probably swimming at about 16 kilometres (10 miles) an hour. It is much harder to go very fast in water than it is on land or in the air.

There are a few fish, however, which can put on real bursts of speed. Some salmon can travel at 40 kilometres (25 miles) an hour. The flying fish, which leaps out of the water and glides for a time on wing-like fins, may reach 56 kilometres (35 miles) an hour. This is probably the top speed for marlin and huge tuna as well. Swordfish and bonito may move a little faster, but just how fast is hard to tell.

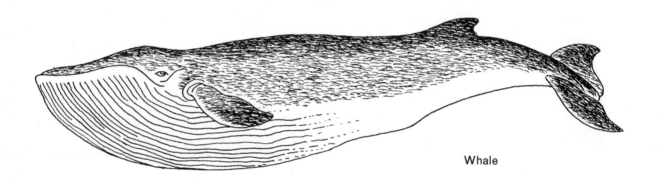

Whale

Dolphins and whales cannot be timed

Dolphins, playful relatives of the porpoises and blue whales, often swim alongside ocean liners. They have been known to swim much faster than modern vessels cruising at 40 kilometres (25 miles) an hour. Nobody knows exactly how fast those little cousins of the whales can travel. In fact, we are not sure of the top speed of the whales themselves. But some whales must be among the fastest swimmers in the ocean, with speeds of about 56 kilometres (35 miles) an hour. It is hard to time them exactly, for if they are followed in a fast boat they may sound, or disappear far beneath the surface, and suddenly change direction underwater.

30

Dolphins sometimes swim for hours just ahead of the bow of a speeding ocean liner. When they tire of the play, they may take off – full speed, straight ahead.

Kangaroos – and their smaller cousins, the wallabies – leap over the Australian plains like giant grasshoppers.

3 Tops in their field

To judge the best jumper study the animal's hind legs

When you look at an animal you can often guess how it lives. A bird with long wings would most likely be a good flyer. A mammal with pointed teeth probably feeds on other animals. The webs of a frog's feet tell you it is a good swimmer.

The best jumpers are usually those with strong hind legs. The frog's

32

hind legs are long and powerful, so it is a good jumper. And both grass-hoppers and kangaroos, noteworthy jumpers in the animal world, have large hind legs.

Animals make better broad jumpers than high jumpers

There are some animals that are high jumpers and some that are broad jumpers. In general, animals can make greater broad jumps than high jumps. This is because an animal can work up a great deal of speed to propel it before a broad jump, but the high-jumping animal is quickly pulled back to earth by the force of gravity.

The high leapers

The highest jumpers do not always have the biggest legs. Aquatic animals such as fish and whales can jump without any legs at all. They use their powerful tails to drive them through the water.

One of the best groups of aquatic leapers is the salmon family. Salmon and trout swim up into small streams and rivers to lay their eggs. Such streams often have waterfalls along the way and the fish must leap the falls to get upstream. Scientists have measured the height to which these fish can jump. Some salmon can leap higher than 3 metres (10 feet). These salmon would be able to jump from the floor of a basketball court, right into the basket!

Whales and dolphins are also great leapers. The bottle-nosed dolphin seems to love to jump out of the water. It quickly learns to leap over a bar or through a hoop. Dolphins have been known to jump 4·5 metres (15 feet) into the air.

Great size does not stop the dolphin's larger relatives from jumping. The hump-back whale (measuring 15·24 metres or 50 feet) sometimes throws itself clear out of the water. It lands with a splash that can be heard miles away.

Among the best high jumpers on land are the deer. Some have been known to jump as high as 2·4 metres (8 feet). Mountain lions may leap even higher – up to 3·65 metres (12 feet) into the air.

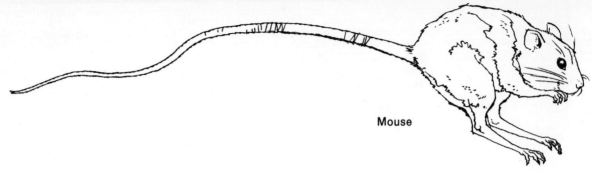

Mouse

Animals have their champion broad jumpers

In measuring jumping ability, the size of the animal must be considered. The 1·82 metres (6 foot) leap of a jumping mouse is not as great as the 3·65 metres (12 foot) leap of the snowshoe hare, but the mouse is not nearly as big as the hare.

It is hard to decide just when an animal has made its greatest effort. Most animals do not enter contests just to see who can win. They run or jump or swim only as fast as necessary. However, some of the best jumps have been measured. Jack rabbits, for instance, have been known to cover 6 metres (20 feet) in a single bound. The large Australian grey kangaroo has a recorded jump of 8 metres (27 feet).

The white-tailed deer has been known to leap farther than 6 metres (20 feet) in one bound. The puma, or mountain lion, often catches deer. It has been known to leap 11·58 metres (38 feet). But perhaps the longest jump of all is made by the African impala. This graceful antelope with the curving horns has been known to leap 12 metres (40 feet)!

The frog may be small, but do not count him out

Generally, the frog is about as good a jumper for its size as almost any animal. Frogs have been known to jump 3·65 metres (12 feet), which is a fair distance for an animal about as large as a man's fist.

An insect was the world's first pole-vaulter

Most creatures are propelled by their legs when they leap. But the tiny collembola, often called a springtail, jumps by means of a little tube, or trigger, beneath its body. This trigger is kept folded under the insect. To leap, the insect releases the trigger, which then snaps backwards. This

34

The graceful impala is the champion African long-jumper.

throws the springtail into the air. The trigger in fact serves the same purpose as a pole-vaulter's pole.

Springtails are small, dark-coloured insects often found floating on the surface of brooks or ponds. Collembola are often found under the bark of trees. Those found on the surface of snow are known as snow fleas. You will recognise them because they hop when disturbed. In spite of their tiny size, they may jump 15 centimetres (6 inches).

Scientists believe that springtails have been on earth for more than 300 million years. This means they were here before the dinosaurs. So they might be called the world's first pole-vaulters.

Strong hind legs enable the grasshopper to jump a metre or more.

It is ability, not size

If size compared with ability, the insects would be the champion jumpers. Grasshoppers have been known to jump a metre (3 feet) or more. Tiny fleas, hopping about on a dog's back, may jump 60 centimetres (2 feet) at a leap.

These may not seem such tremendous hops until the size of the animal is considered in relation to the distance it can jump. If a deer could jump as far for its size as a flea, it would be able to jump the length of six football fields in a single bound – a length of some 547 metres (1,800 feet).

36

The mystery of the Mexican jumping bean

Actually, Mexican jumping beans are not beans at all. They are really the seeds of a plant related to the poinsettia. They may be attacked by the caterpillar of a little moth, which makes its home inside the seeds. When the caterpillar moves, the seed moves, too. The bean does not really jump, of course, but rolls around when its little inhabitant changes position.

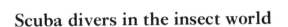

Diving Beetle

Scuba divers in the insect world

There are a number of insects which take air with them beneath the surface. They might be compared to little scuba divers. Two familiar kinds are water boatmen and diving beetles.

When these insects come up to the surface, they gather a bubble of air in a mat of special hairs on their bodies. Then, when they dive again, the bubble remains caught in the hair. Water boatmen look as if they are clothed in silver because of the air film that surrounds the back portion of their bodies. Diving beetles appear to be carrying a shiny piece of metal near their hind legs.

The creature that builds its own diving bell

A diving bell is used by divers to hold air for underwater breathing. The diving spider makes its own air-filled bell by weaving a net of silk. It attaches this silk to the stems of underwater plants. Then, carrying down bubbles caught between a few strands of silk, it releases them under the bell. The spider does this until it has enough air to form a dry room under the water. There it lives and raises its young.

The depth of animal dives

It is even more difficult to measure the deepest dive of an animal than it is to measure its highest speed or greatest leap. However, a few swimming animals have become tangled in nets set for fish, and it is possible to work out how deep the swimmer was by knowing the depth of the net that trapped it.

Canvasback ducks have been caught at about 24 metres (80 feet) beneath the water. Loons and grebes have gone down to 30 metres (100 feet). One loon was known to dive more than 60 metres (200 feet). Of course, deeper dives have probably not been observed by man. The sperm whale dives deep in search of giant squids. It may go down to 305 metres (1000 feet) or more, staying under water for as long as half an hour.

Perhaps the deepest dive a whale has been known to make was that of a sperm whale found off the coast of South America. It became tangled in an undersea cable. The cable was lying on the bottom of the ocean at the time – more than 1,064 metres (3,500 feet) down!

Their special breathing apparatus prevents whales from suffocating during long periods under water

Man has an automatic breathing system. If you try to hold your breath longer than about a minute, an automatic response, which is governed by the amount of the waste gas carbon dioxide in the blood, forces you to exhale. But, on the other hand, the whale's breathing is not entirely controlled by this response.

Scientists know some of the things that happen when a whale dives. On many whales a flap closes the blowhole, or breathing entrance, so that water cannot get in by mistake, even under great pressure. The heartbeat slows down, thus slowing down the transport of carbon dioxide. And the whale's automatic breathing device stops functioning so that it does not have to gasp for breath when carbon dioxide builds up in the blood.

This seems to work very well for the whale. This big animal has been known to stay under water for more than an hour.

High marks for these four-legged swimmers

Sea mammals seem to be the champions in this class. Next to the whales in swimming ability come the seals, sea lions and walruses. Many of them are so perfectly fitted for a life in the water that they can hardly get about on land. But the legs of these mammals are so much like fins that they can hardly be called true four-legged animals. In fact, their scientific name, Pinnipedia, means fin-footed.

The prize for the best four-legged swimmer, then, would go to the otter. It is such an expert at swimming and diving that it is often called a fish in fur. This big cousin of the weasel and mink is as much at home in the water as it is on the land. It can, if necessary, stay under water for five minutes. In the winter, it can stay hidden beneath the ice even longer. The otter blows a bubble, which rises and collects under the ice. Then it comes back to breathe the bubble two or three times before finally having to inhale fresh new air.

When an otter swims under water its soft, thick fur traps a layer of air, making it appear as if clothed in silver.

Emperor penguins of the Antarctic are clumsy on land, but among the
most graceful of birds underwater.

Underwater birds that fly

A penguin walking on land looks as if it were going to fall down any minute.
Its webbed feet shuffle along and its stubby little wings stick out as if
trying to keep balance. Sometimes it steps on its own toes!

In the water, however, the penguin is a wonderful swimmer. Its wings
become graceful fins; the webbed feet turn out to be the best of rudders.
The penguin can twist and turn as it follows its fish dinner. Flapping its
wings, it seems to fly under water.

Loons, grebes, auks, puffins and some kinds of diving ducks also use
their wings under water.

40

Birds that are called hell-divers

The fast-diving water birds known as loons and grebes look rather like ducks with pointed bills. They float in the water, keeping a watchful eye out for enemies. At any sudden motion along the shore, they may dive beneath the water's surface. So quick are they at diving that hunters usually cannot shoot them. Seeing the flash of the gun, the birds disappear before the bullet reaches them.

Animal knot-makers

Members of the snake family are, of course, the best equipped for twisting their bodies into knots. Eels are able to tie these knots too.

Perhaps the best of all knot-makers is a little creature known as the hairworm, horsehair worm, or Gordian worm. This worm may be a little thicker than a sewing thread, and 20 or 25 centimetres (8 or 10 inches) long. The hairworms live most of their lives inside the bodies of insects. Superstitious people have long thought this tiny worm to be a horsehair that has come to life.

Gordian worms may tie themselves in such tight knots that they are little more than a ball. This ball may seem to have no beginning or end, but somewhere inside are to be found the head and tail of the strange horsehair worm.

The eel can outwit the fisherman

As slippery as an eel is a good description of these snake-like fish. But if an eel is caught on a hook, its slippery slime is of little use in helping it to get away.

The eel has a trick which often works, however. It quickly throws its body into a simple knot. Passing this knot forward along its body, it finally pulls its head through. Then it tightens the knot down on the fishing line. If the hook is not embedded too deeply it may pull right out of the eel's mouth. Sometimes the eel will even break the line.

The strongest animals perform unbelievable tasks

Highest honours for strength would undoubtedly go to the great whales. It takes tremendous power to propel their huge bodies through water. One blue whale pulled a 27-metre (90-foot) whaling ship through the water for eight hours at a speed of about 8 kilometres (5 miles) an hour. And all the time the ship's engines churning at full speed, were heading in the opposite direction.

The strongest land animals are the elephants. When they are tamed, they can be used to move objects weighing several tonnes. Male African elephants often have to carry heavy loads for much of their adult lives, for their tusks alone have been known to have a total weight of 135 kilograms (300 pounds).

People often think of gorillas as having great strength. Although they are powerful creatures, they are not as savage as explorers once thought they were. They live in their native African forests in peaceful groups, seldom disturbing their neighbours.

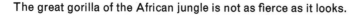

The great gorilla of the African jungle is not as fierce as it looks.

This scarab beetle rolls a ball of dung which is bigger than itself.

Insects really can carry twenty times their own weight

The strength of many insects is surprising. Sexton beetles, which bury the bodies of dead animals as food for their young, are only medium-sized insects. Yet they can burrow under the body of a mouse many times their size and push it along to a different position.

The beetles are the largest order of insects, with about 250,000 species, and some of the most interesting are the scarab beetles. They were regarded by the ancient Egyptians as sacred creatures. They all feed on dung which they roll into balls and in which the female sometimes lays its eggs.

Leaf-cutting ants carry big pieces of leaves to the nest. These leaves serve as gardens on which the ants grow mushrooms for food. Sometimes these pieces of leaf may weigh twenty times as much as the ant.

Leaf-cutting ants cut chunks of leaves and carry them, like green flags, back to their underground nest.

Small size and muscle composition make insects strong

Feats of strength are common in the insect world. This is not as strange as it may seem. The huge dinosaurs were so heavy that some of them had to float in water much of the time. It must have taken great effort just to move on dry land. The great blue whale of today could not live out of water for even a few minutes; the weight of its huge body would crush its lungs.

Insects, however, are so tiny that they seem to have no weight at all. Their outer skins, or coverings, are strong supports for hundreds of muscles. This combination of many muscles with small size makes insects tremendously powerful. If a grown man were as strong for his size, he could carry his motor-car around on his back.

The rattlesnake wrestle

It would seem impossible for an animal without arms or legs to have a wrestling match, but rattlesnakes do not let the lack of limbs hinder their wrestling.

Since rattlesnakes are not greatly affected by their own poison, they have to have some other way to settle disputes. If two snakes claim the same territory, the argument may be settled by a wrestling match. Each snake rears its head and neck as high as possible and tries to force the other snake to the ground – in a way similar to the game of arm wrestling.

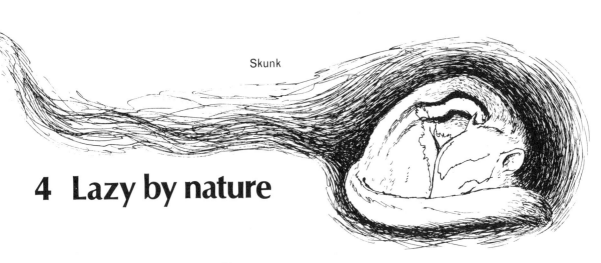

Skunk

4 Lazy by nature

The animal's need to hibernate

The death sleep is the name that is sometimes given to hibernation. The heart slows down to just a few beats per minute. Blood circulates so slowly that a cut will not bleed. The hibernating animal hardly seems to be breathing at all. Its body temperature drops far below normal.

Hibernation is nature's way of helping an animal to get through the winter. If it remained active, it would need to find food to keep alive. Buried in its den, however, it lives on the fat which it has stored on its body.

Winter sleeps vary

The duration of winter sleep, or hibernation, depends on the kind of animal. It also depends on how much fat it was able to store up before it went into its winter sleep.

Bears do not really hibernate at all. They go to sleep for a while, but their heartbeat, temperature and breathing rate stay close to normal. Skunks and raccoons may sleep for a month or longer at a time, coming out of the den when a winter thaw warms them. Hedgehogs roll themselves up in nests of dry leaves for the winter. Bats will hibernate in a cave or an old, deserted building. Although squirrels sleep more than usual they do not truly hibernate.

Sometimes a warm day will wake a hibernating animal. Melting snow may run down into its burrow. Then it stirs for a few hours before going back to sleep.

Those large dark eyes of the dormouse are open only about half the time. It spends six months of the year curled up in sleep.

The animal that hibernates the longest

Perhaps the best hibernator of all is the European dormouse. In late summer it puts on such a layer of fat that it waddles when it walks.

By September the dormouse is often ready to hibernate. Even though the weather may still be warm, it curls up in its nest. It often hibernates until April – six months later. The dormouse may spend half its life sleeping.

46

Some animals hibernate in summer

Summer sleep is called aestivation. Some desert animals aestivate when the summer weather gets too dry and hot. Desert mice may spend weeks in summer sleep. Tortoises go deep into their burrows and sleep until the weather is better.

Even when their ponds dry up, some fish can live

There are a few fish that can live out of water. But if a pond dries up, most of the fish will die.

Bullheads can burrow into the mud and keep alive as long as their skin is moist. Carp and goldfish can live for days in water that is little more than liquid mud.

The lungfishes of Africa, South America and Australia can do even better. When the pond begins to dry up, they make a little chamber of slime and mud. They then gulp air through a little hole in the chamber. The air goes to a sac in their bodies which serves as a lung. The fish can remain in their chamber for weeks while their pond is parched and dry in the tropical heat.

Goldfish

Bears give birth to their babies while they are asleep

Many animals make a special nest in which to have their babies. But bears merely find a good place to sleep during the cold season. Then, some time in the late winter, the cubs are born to the drowsy mother bear. She hardly knows they are there.

The young bears are as hungry as any babies. They nurse on their mother, while she is still wholly or partly asleep, until she finally wakes up and actively takes care of them herself.

A grizzly bear turns over a stone to find food for her cubs.

Horses do sleep standing up

If you have ever seen a horse drowsing in the middle of a pasture, you know it can, indeed, sleep on its feet. So can zebras and donkeys. When one of these creatures really wants to relax, however, it lies down like other animals.

One animal never closes its eyes

It seems strange that any creature is incapable of closing its eyes even once during its lifetime, but this is just what happens to every snake. Instead of eyelids as a protection for its eyes, a snake's eyes have a clear, transparent covering. When a snake sheds its skin, the eye covering goes with it. A new covering just beneath the old one takes its place.

How can a snake sleep? Apparently, it somehow does not see anything with those wide-open eyes when it is asleep. Snakes curled up in the sun with their eyes open will often not notice someone coming until the ground nearby is tapped or their bodies are touched.

A scientific view on the value of Ground Hog Day

In America the woodchuck or ground hog may come out on 2nd February, which is known as Ground Hog Day, or he may sleep a few weeks longer. The ground hog can wake up at any time. Often, however, in some parts of the United States, there is a thaw around the first week of February. During this thaw, the ground hog may stretch, yawn and poke his nose outside for an afternoon.

An old superstition says that if he sees his shadow, he will be frightened and run back to his hole. Then he will sleep six more weeks until spring comes.

But if the sun is not shining, the ground hog will not see his shadow. He will not go back to sleep, and spring will have arrived. Of course, there is no truth in this belief. But, after a long winter, it is fun to think of the first ground hog of spring.

This animal is carried around by his mate

Although the ground hog appears the laziest of animals with all his sleeping, the male angler fish does even less work. He swims through the ocean until he finds his mate. She is several times larger than he is. He attaches himself to her so firmly that he comes to look like a little bump growing out of her body. There he will stay for the rest of his life. A male angler fish does not even bother to feed himself. He merely absorbs food from the bloodstream of his mate.

Lazy people are called drones because of their similarity to certain insects

The males of most common species of ants, bees and wasps do not do any work around the nest. They could not work if they wanted to – their jaws and bodies are not strong enough for the many jobs that must be done. The male bees and wasps do not even have a sting to protect themselves.

The job of a drone is to mate with a female, or queen, so that she may lay her eggs. The actual work of the nest is done by the workers, which are also females. Probably every bee you see in a flower and every ant on a pavement is a female. She gathers the food, protects the nest and even feeds the drones.

Some female animals let their mates care for the young

Although drones may seem to do little work, there are some males which carry on the household duties all by themselves. The male stickleback fish builds a little nest in a brook. He chases a female into the nest and keeps her there until she lays her eggs. Then he chases her away and raises the babies himself.

The male mouth-breeder catfish carries the eggs around in his mouth. He does not eat at all until after they have hatched.

The female of the giant water bug catches the male after mating. Then, while he struggles to get away, she lays her eggs on his back.

Seahorses are strange little fish. They swim in an upright position,
hang on with their tails – and the male carries his mate's eggs.

Another aquatic baby sitter is the male seahorse. He carries the eggs of
his mate in a stomach pouch like a little kangaroo. Then, when it is time for
them to hatch, he gives birth to the babies.

Cowbird

There are birds that lay their eggs in the nests of other birds

The European cuckoo and the American cowbird make other birds care for their young. Stealing to the nest of a smaller bird, they lay an egg and quickly fly away.

Sometimes the smaller bird will desert the nest when she finds the strange egg. Or she may build a whole new nest over the top of the egg. Many times, however, she will raise the stranger as her own. He is usually larger and faster growing than her other babies and may often push them right out of the nest.

There are a few other birds that have this habit. The reasons behind this behaviour are not always clear, but scientists think they know why the cowbird leaves her eggs in another bird's nest. For centuries, the ancestors of the cowbird wandered on the prairies with the American bison, feeding on insects stirred up from the grass by this shaggy mammal. The cowbird could not very well have a nest and still stay with the bison. So she gave other birds the job of caring for her young. They became the cowbird's unwilling baby sitters.

The living habits of commensals

The word commensal means sharing the same table. There are many animals which share each other's food. Certain ants pass drops of sweet nectar from one to the other. A little mite, which looks like a tiny spider,

52

often lives in the ant nest. When the drop is passed, the mite pokes its beak into the sweet liquid and helps itself – like an extra straw in an ice cream shake.

Some crabs have sea anemones growing on their backs. The sea anemone is an animal which looks like a plant. Its appearance helps to camouflage the crab. The petals of the sea anemone are really arms loaded with stinging cells. When the crab finds a snail or when the sea anemone stings a fish, there will be food for both of them.

One kind of crab lives right inside the shell of an oyster. It stays there all its life, feeding on material which comes in with the water the oyster takes into its shell.

Tiny protozoans live in the bodies of termites. They help digest the wood which the termites eat.

A little fish called the remora, or shark sucker, often attaches itself to the shark by a suction cup on its head. When the shark catches some food, the remora swims around and helps itself to the pieces.

How parasites make a living

Some parasites, like the flea, hop around from one animal to another. They feed on the blood of whichever dog or cat happens to be their home for the moment.

Other parasites are far less active – they must be carried around. Tapeworms live inside some other animal, which is known as a host, and do not have to get their own food. They never have any worries about heat or cold, rain or snow.

Life is not always easy for parasites, however. If a flea bites too hard, the dog will scratch and nip until it kills the little pest. Ticks which attack a a rhinoceros may be found and eaten by the tick bird, which rides along on the back of the great beast.

When the host of a parasite dies, the parasite may die, too. Many parasites produce hundreds of thousands of young, but only a few ever find their way to a new host. The rest of them die shortly after they are born.

5 Each has its own way

Busy as a beaver really is true

The beaver always seems to be working. It adds some sticks or mud to its lodge, or house. Then it swims over to inspect the dam it has built. It makes little canals to float tree limbs to its pond. These limbs come from trees it has cut down with its sharp teeth.

The beaver, which lives in North America, is so good at building dams and canals that it is called the engineer in a fur coat.

Beavers do not sleep during the winter; they remain active all year. There is a good reason for all this activity. A good-sized beaver may weigh 9 kilograms (20 pounds) or more. It takes a lot of food to keep it going until spring. But the beaver can store plenty to eat. When the pond is frozen, it feeds on the bark and buds of the limbs it has stuck in the mud beneath the ice. It is one of the few animals that actually becomes fat in winter.

Humming-bird

The humming-bird's hum is not a song

If you have ever watched a humming-bird as it flew from one flower to another, perhaps you have heard its hum. This noise is not the humming-bird's song, however. It is made by the rapid beat of the tiny bird's wings. Its real song is little more than a squeak.

The wings of this little animal go so fast that they appear blurred. It beats its wings as many as 75 times a second – more than 4,000 times a minute!

Insects that live in waterfalls and river rapids

There are several animals that live in the rapids of the swiftest rivers. All their lives they are surrounded by tumbling, rushing water.

The young of the black fly live right on the surface of rocks in the rapids. Some of them spin a strong thread by which they attach themselves to the rocks. If the thread should break, they would be washed away in an instant. Some kinds of insects glue themselves to a rock and then make little nets to help strain food from the rushing water. The young stone flies are flat, with clinging legs. They crawl over rocks and pebbles in the swiftest water and somehow manage to keep from being washed away.

The bird that walks on the bottom of mountain streams

The bird with this strange habit is the water ouzel, or dipper, of western North America. It is about the size of a robin, but with a short tail. It is surprising to see how the brown bird can walk right into the foaming rapids and disappear. Somehow, it clings to the rocks beneath the water, where it catches insects and small fish.

The surf is home for these animals

Probably one of the strangest places to live is in the world of crashing ocean waves. But, of course, it is not strange to the creatures that spend their lives there. Some of the more interesting of the many creatures living there are the sand bug, the acorn barnacle and the grunion.

The sand bug is also known as the Hippa or sand mole. It is not a bug or mole at all, however, but a crustacean. This means that it is covered with a crust, like the crab and the lobster. About the size and shape of an olive, it lives in the sand at the point where the waves come crashing down. With each wave, it is tumbled wildly through the water. Little feathery bristles near its mouth serve as strainers to catch other creatures which are tossed about by the same wave. As the wave recedes, the bug quickly burrows into the sand to await the next wave.

Acorn barnacles look like halves of white acorns that are stuck to the rocks. With each wave the acorn opens up and several feathery nets reach out into the water. Scooping quickly, they pull in any food washed around by the waves.

The grunion is a little fish of the Pacific coast. During the strongest tides, the spring tides, the grunions are washed ashore by the thousand. They lay their eggs in that part of the sand reached only by the highest waves. Then, battered and tumbled by the sea, they dash back as quickly as they can to the safety of deep water. Two weeks later, their young hatch and are washed out of the sand by the returning spring tides.

Sanderlings

Watch the sanderling search for food and know why this wading bird is called the sea foam bird

The little sanderling seems to be always on the go. The sanderling is about the size of a robin and is light in colour. It follows each wave up and down sandy beaches, keeping just ahead of the water as the wave crashes, and running back down when the wave recedes.

From a distance, sanderlings look like flecks of foam washing back and forth at the edge of each wave. But as you watch them, you discover what they are doing – you see why they keep so close to the moving water. Their little black bills keep poking into the sand as they run. They are looking for food, which is the sand bugs and other creatures that have been washed up by the waves. They must hurry, or their food will burrow down deep into the sand again.

The peacock proudly displays his gorgeous feathers.

Courtship dances and ritual fighting

There is usually a distinct difference between the appearance of male and female birds. The males are generally larger, with more elaborate body structure, a greater variety of plumage and much more brilliant colours. These differences are best seen in such birds as peacocks, pheasants and birds of paradise, where the male is noted for his striking feathers, and the female is often drab and ordinary by comparison.

The male bird uses his feathers to attract the female and display his strength and handsome appearance. These displays are very spectacular. They sometimes lead to courtship dances between the males and females which follow a set and complicated ritual. Their purpose seems to be to establish some form of mutual trust and harmony before mating.

There are also threat displays in which rival males posture and even fight one another, usually over territory, although some people still hold to the old belief that males fight for the favours of a chosen mate.

Bats

The flyer that needs a warm-up

Most birds and insects are ready to fly at any moment. But just as many aeroplanes and motor-cars are warmed up before they are used to help their engines to be at their best, bats often need to warm up for a while before an evening's flight. They have been hanging to the wall of a cave or inside a hollow tree all day, and may actually be several degrees cooler than normal. So they make a few practice flights. Then, when their temperature rises, they dash out into the evening air.

As blind as a bat is not altogether true

The expression 'blind as a bat' is not usually true. Many of these creatures can see very well, but their eyesight is of little value to them after dark.

Bats find their way by making a series of high-pitched squeaks. The echo from these squeaks warns the bat what lies ahead of him in the gloom. With his echo-locator he can tell the difference between a flying moth and a tree branch. He can even fly in a darkened room strung with many wires without bumping into them.

The bat's sound-location sense is amazingly accurate. High-speed motion pictures have shown that a bat catches insects with its mouth. If it misses an insect in flight, it may reach out with a wing-tip or the web on one of its hind feet – and catch its food without pausing.

When a busy spot is called a beehive, it is suitably named

There is always something doing in a beehive – even during the winter. In coldest weather the bees cluster together, buzzing their wings to keep warm. They may form a ball of hundreds of bees. As the ones in the centre of the ball get warm, they move towards the outside. This keeps the temperature of the hive well above freezing point.

As soon as the weather gets warm in spring, the hive buzzes with activity. Some workers carry out the old bees that have died during the winter. Others repair the combs, making new cells both for honey and for the eggs which the queen will produce. Still others fly out in search of the early spring flowers. From these they will gather nectar for honey and pollen for food.

From this time until it again becomes quiet during the winter, the beehive will be a scene of constant activity. Even at night the faint hum of the insects can be heard near a beehive.

Honeybees are among the few insects that are active all year round.

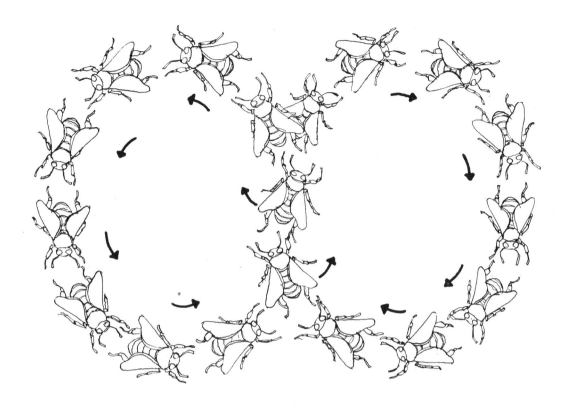

The dance of the bees has a special meaning

When a bee finds a good supply of nectar, she gathers as much as she can. Then she flies in a circle round the clump of flowers. This probably helps her to remember exactly where they are.

Back at the hive, she goes into a strange dance. First she circles one way and then the other. Then she walks in a straight line, wagging her body like the tail of a little dog.

Dr Karl von Frisch of Germany discovered the meaning of this dance of the bees. The circles tell how far away the flowers are. The greater the number of circles, the farther away are the flowers. The tail-wagging line tells the other bees in what direction to fly. And the scent of the nectar still on the dancing bee tells the others what kind of flowers to look for.

Many other bees, following the same steps, are soon doing the dance. Then they fly away. They go straight to the blossoms, even though they have never seen them before.

61

This bird skims its food from the water's surface

Little fish and small crustaceans stay near the top of the water. This may help them escape the large fish below, but it is no protection from the beak of the black skimmer.

Flying along just above the surface, the skimmer drops its lower jaw into the water. Back and forth it goes, scooping up any unlucky creatures near the surface before they can dive.

Swallows and swifts in flight scoop water from a pond

Although swallows and swifts have long, pointed wings and are wonderful flyers, their feet are extremely short and weak and they can hardly walk on land. The wings of some swifts are so long that they have difficulty getting into the air from a flat surface and their insect food is caught entirely on the wing.

With such short legs, these birds usually perch on a tree limb or telephone wire so that they can get into flight again. Instead of landing near a puddle to drink, they often skim water from the surface of a pond or stream while still on the wing.

The stoop of a hawk

One of the most thrilling sights in nature is that of the stoop, or steep dive of the hawk on its prey. Not all hawks stoop. The hawk-like peregrine falcon, however, may dive with such speed that the whistling of the wind in its half-closed wings can be heard from a great distance. It hits its prey with terrific force, often killing it with a blow of its clenched foot as it speeds by.

Such a dive can be made only in mid-air. The falcon cannot dive full-speed at something on the ground. Flying ducks are able to escape the hawk, provided it is seen in time, by dropping to a pond below. There they would be safe, because a hawk's dive is so rapid that it would carry it right into the pond.

62

Beak and claws, plus great speed, enable the hawk to catch its prey.

The gannets in bird city, of Quebec's Bonaventure Island, plunge head first off the cliffs for their dinners.

Birds that dive full speed into the water

There is one hawk which plunges right into the water. This is the osprey, or fish hawk. It hovers high in the air until it spots a fish. Then, closing its wings, it plunges downward and hits the water with a tremendous splash. Usually, the osprey comes up with a fish in its talons. Sometimes the fish is so large that it cannot be carried away. Then flapping its wings in the air and dragging the fish through the water, the osprey tows it to shore.

Pelicans crash into the water so hard that it is a wonder they do not break their necks.

But one of the most surprising sights is the plunge of the gannets. These white, sharp-beaked birds, sometimes called sea geese, make their nests high on cliffs at the edge of the ocean. When a school of fish is sighted, they jump right off their cliff. Down they drop, 30 metres (100 feet) or more, landing headfirst in the cold water far below. And they may continue on down until they are 15 metres (50 feet) below the surface.

How the dragonfly gets its name

One of the most ferocious insects in nature is also one of the commonest and can probably be found no more than a kilometre or two from most people. This is the flying dragon, or dragonfly. Millions of years ago, there were dragonflies measuring more than 30 centimetres (1 foot) in length which had wing-spans of about 60 centimetres (2 feet). Although today's dragonflies are seldom more than a few centimetres long, they still must be a fearsome sight to a mosquito.

Today, you can see dragonflies speeding over the water of the ponds in parks, or almost any other pool in the city or country. If you were to follow one closely, you would see that it is well named. Dragonflies carry their legs laced together, like a little basket. As they fly, they catch mosquitoes and gnats in the basket. Then they pass them forward to their mouth. Any time one of these insects is flying, it is probably eating – and it is flying most of the time.

This creature even begins life resembling a dragon. When it is an underwater nymph, it creeps up on small fish and tadpoles. A special lower lip, hinged like a folding door, shoots out when it is close enough to its victim. At the end of this lip is a pair of tongs. These catch the unlucky victim and bring it back to the waiting jaws. Sometimes a dragonfly nymph shoots after its prey by squirting water out from its rear. This gives it a thrust like a jet plane.

Wolverine

Wolverine – the glutton of the north

Able to run almost as fast as a rabbit, to fight like a bear and climb like a cat, the wolverine is an animal tornado. Even though it is little more than 91 centimetres (3 feet) long, it can beat almost any animal in a fight.

Wolverines live in many of the far-northern countries of the world. They eat almost anything they can find: insects, meat, berries and fish. They will even rush in and chase a wolf or lynx away from a meal. If any food is left after they have finished eating, they may cover it with a bad-smelling secretion from their own bodies. Such a creature, wanting every bit of food in sight, is well-named the glutton of the north.

If enemies do not bother the wolverine, why aren't the northern forests full of them? One reason is that wolverines seem unable to stand each other! If they happen to meet, one of them will usually move far away. One wolverine in several square miles of forest seems to be enough.

The pygmy hippopotamus likes to be alone

Hippopotamuses are generally very sociable animals and like to live close together in small family herds. Usually one male dominates an area of land and gathers his family of females and young ones about him. Although a hippopotamus will attack fiercely any male attempting to enter his ground, each group lives quite peaceably within sight of the other, minding its own business.

About one-tenth the size of a full-grown hippopotamus, the little pygmy hippo lives by rivers in West Africa, although it does not often enter the water. It is a solitary animal and is rarely seen in company.

66

Despite its ferocious-looking teeth the pygmy hippo is not much bigger than a large pig.

The shrew is a living whirlwind

The shrew seems to do everything at top speed. Its heart may beat 500 times a minute, and its breathing may be half that rate. If you hold a shrew in your hand, you get a strange sensation, as if you were holding some kind of buzzing bee. Its little heart and its breathing are going so fast that the shrew vibrates like a machine.

A shrew may have half a dozen babies in a litter, and three or four litters of babies in a single year. The baby shrews grow so fast that they may be out of the nest in three weeks.

Shrews are always hungry. They will eat snails, insects, frogs and birds' eggs. Even though many shrews are smaller than mice, they will attack animals several times their size. They may even attack each other. And, of course, they do not hibernate – they could never put on enough fat for even two nights' sleep. In fact, shrews have been known to starve overnight for lack of food.

One scientist wanted to raise a family of shrews. He put a male and female shrew in a large container with what he thought was plenty of food. But the next day, all the food, and only one very fat shrew was left.

Shrew

One of the most startling sounds in the forest is the snort of a white-tailed deer, the commonest species of deer in North America. Here a buck is seen with its antlers still in their velvety covering. A new set of antlers is grown each year.

6 Animal sounds and their meaning

Different animals have different reasons for the noise they make

A great many animals can make some sound or other. They may purr, scream, growl, sing, chirp, buzz, drum or coo. Some of these noises are so loud that we can hardly stand them. Others are so soft that they can just barely be heard by human ears. And still others are pitched so high or so low that we cannot hear them at all without the use of special listening devices.

There are a number of reasons why animals have these varieties of sound. One animal sings to attract a mate. Another sings to warn other animals to keep away from its nesting territory. The white-tailed deer may snort when an enemy surprises it. A gorilla beats its chest when it is ready to fight or to flee. Beavers slap their tails, rabbits thump the ground and woodchucks whistle. Each of them has a special reason for a special note.

Happy as a lark may not be exactly true

The skylark is probably the best known bird to fit this description, singing its song high in the air over the meadow. But the lark may not be happy at all. It may not be unhappy either. Birds probably do not have times of joy and sadness as people do.

Human beings can build fences around their land. The song of a bird is often just the bird's way of putting up a boundary around the area which he claims as his own. He is telling others of his species that this is his own private territory.

Lark

The loudness of a bird's song does not always indicate its size

Just as it is important to remember size difference when judging how far an animal can jump, size must be considered when deciding how loud a bird can sing.

When you listen to the sound of the South American bellbird, or cotinga, you feel that this bird must be at least as big as a chicken. But it is actually not much larger than a robin. Yet so loud is its clear, ringing note that it is almost painful to be near it when one of these birds is singing close at hand. The call of this feathered songster can be heard half a kilometre away. It is one of the loudest singers known for its size.

The kookaburra bird of Australia is another great noise-maker. Its call sounds like human laughter or the braying of a donkey. For this reason, it is often called a laughing jackass. The kookaburra can be heard nearly a kilometre away. Its size matches its voice, for this bird may be larger than a crow. The bugle of the whooping crane can be heard for about 2 kilo-

The kookaburra is called the laughing jackass because its loud call sounds like human laughter. It catches snakes and other animals as food.

The rare whooping crane is tall enough to look a boy or girl right in the eye. It makes a loud, bugling noise which sounds like someone trying to play the trumpet.

metres ($1\frac{1}{2}$ miles) when conditions are right, but the whooping crane is much larger than most other birds. A whooping crane may stand more than 1 metre (4 feet) high on its long slender legs. Its wings may extend more than 2 metres (7 feet) when in flight.

One of the world's rarest birds, the whooping crane is almost pure white, with black wing tips. Its loud call echoes over the marshes of its winter grounds in Texas and its summer breeding grounds in Canada. Perhaps it has been this very distinctive call which has brought it to the attention of hunters.

72

Some birds can be felt rather than heard

A number of birds make noises with their wings. Goldeneye ducks are sometimes called whistlers because of the sound of the air rushing through their wings in flight. The male woodcock flies in a spiral path, his wings making a chirping sound as they catch the air. Pigeons and doves too, make a whistling sound as they fly.

The ruffed grouse of the woodlands, however, makes more noise with his wings than almost any other bird. Finding a big log, he stands on top of it and beats his wings violently. The motion is almost the same as if he were clapping his hands. The dull thumping sound is felt in the air, rather than heard. You can feel a grouse a kilometre away on a quiet day in the woods.

The American Indians used to call a grouse the beating heart of the forest. They could sometimes attract a grouse by striking their chests with their fists. The grouse, hearing the thumping sound, would come to chase this invader.

Like a small turkey, the ruffed grouse spreads its tail feathers to attract its mate. On a spring day in the woods you may hear it drumming with its wings.

The best bird drummers

The prize for the best drummer would probably go to the woodpecker. Not only does it drill into the wood of trees to get insects for food, but it also taps on hollow limbs as a mating call.

One of the signs of spring in the northern zones is the drumming sound of a woodpecker, sometimes occurring as early as January or February. Its mating call, or tattoo, is much louder than its regular hammering for insects. Sometimes it even drums on a tin roof.

Animals have a special way of saying keep out

The rabbit thumps with his hind feet as a warning to other rabbits to keep out of his territory. He also thumps as a danger signal when enemies are near.

Mice patter the ground rapidly with their front feet for much the same reason. Sometimes, if they are in dry leaves, they sound like rattlesnakes. Many a poisonous snake has turned out to be a harmless mouse.

Nearly everyone knows that a skunk has a terrible weapon in its scent glands. But the skunk is a peaceful animal, and would rather not fight. So if it is disturbed, it may drum rapidly with its front feet. For most animals this is all the warning that is needed. Hearing those feet, they quickly discover something to do a long distance away.

The male spider had better use a drum

Many female spiders are bigger and stronger than the males of their species. Often they will attack their mates. Apparently, part of the reason is that they do not recognise them in time as other spiders.

Wolf spiders usually do not build a web. They wander over leaves and grass, looking for insects to eat. If the male spider did not identify himself, he might be eaten, too. Luckily, he drums on the ground every few seconds with his palps, special little structures near his mouth. Then, as he approaches his ferocious mate, she knows who he is.

74

Many woodpeckers lack musical voices. They drum on old logs, the sides of buildings and even tin roofs to call their mates.

Insects need no musical training for the noises they make

Actually, no insect can really sing. True singing is done with the mouth. The sounds that an insect makes are really buzzes or hums made with other parts of the body.

Insects produce their noises in a number of ways. Some rub that portion of one wing called a file, on the scraper of the other wing. If you should disturb an ant hill and then bend down to listen, you may sometimes make out a very faint squeaking sound. This sound is made as the ants grind their jaws together.

Best among insect music-makers

The most musical group is the grasshopper family. Some grasshoppers rub one leg on another, or on the sides of the body. All we can hear is a faint whisper of sound, but it seems to be enough to be heard by other grasshoppers. Several may sing in perfect time with each other even though they are many yards apart.

Other grasshoppers buzz their wings in flight or even drum on a grass blade with their hind feet.

Katydids, or bush-crickets, and other long-horned grasshoppers make the grasslands noisy with their sounds. They sing by raising their wings and scratching one over the other.

Crickets rub their wings back and forth over each other so quickly that the wings become a blur. The cheerful call of a cricket may continue all winter if it is in the warm cellar of a building. Mole crickets even sing underground.

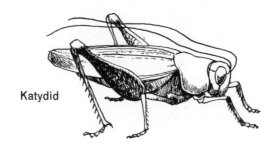

Katydid

Sometimes a mole cricket may cross a country road. Most of the time, however, it stays hidden in the soil.

The message of the cricket's song

The warmer it is, the faster an insect will move and sing. The snowy tree cricket, a little, greenish-white insect about an inch long, is very sensitive to the temperature. It often sits on the bark of a tree or in a bush. There it sings a single, high-pitched, steady musical note. The warmer the day, the faster the tree cricket sings.

It is believed by some people that if you can identify the note of the snowy tree cricket, then count the number of times it sings in fifteen seconds and add forty, the resulting sum is the approximate Fahrenheit temperature.

Insects have ears where you would never expect them

Insects may have their ears in strange places. None of them seems to have them on the sides of the head, where human ears are. Katydids, for example, have theirs on their front legs. Their ears, actually are little flat spots which vibrate with the noise of a singing insect. Other members of the grasshopper family have their ears on the body, under the wings, or in the chest region.

Strangest of all, perhaps, is that scientists have been unable to find any ears at all for the snowy tree cricket. It seems that the female cannot in fact hear her mate's singing. But when he lifts his wings to sing, a gland on his body is uncovered. This gland releases an odour which attracts the female. So even though she cannot hear him, she may come when he calls.

The deathwatch beetle

Superstitious people believe that the sound of the deathwatch beetle means that someone in the family is about to die. But the little insect, usually hidden in the walls of old buildings cannot, of course, predict the future.

The deathwatch beetle tunnels through the wood of old houses and often makes the worm holes which you may see in antique timbers. It makes the noise by striking its head against the sides of its burrow. In a quiet room the sound of this little insect is like the ticking of a watch. It is possible the beetle may make the noise as a means of communicating with others of its kind.

The puzzle of the cicada's song

A cicada, or harvest fly, is often called a locust, but the true locusts are really grasshoppers. Cicadas sing with a loud ringing buzz from the tops of trees in July and August.

It is still a puzzle as to why cicadas sing. Like the snowy tree cricket, they do not seem to have any ears. Only the males sing – and their mates apparently do not even know they are singing!

Perhaps scientists will eventually find that tree crickets and cicadas have ears after all. Until then, the reason for all the noise remains a mystery.

Farmers call the cicadas harvest flies, as they sing at the time of ripening crops.

A talking woodpile means trouble

Sometimes a forester will give a pile of logs a good whack with the side of his axe. Then he will listen. He hopes to hear only silence.

If the wood has been piled up for a long period, however, he may start the logs talking. Wood is often attacked by wood-boring insects which tunnel through it and decrease its value. The sudden blow of the axe will set the borers to striking their heads against the sides of their tunnels. The forester can tell by the sound how badly the insects have attacked the wood.

Sometimes, if he stands quietly, a forester can hear the borers working. The crunch of their jaws as they bite through the wood can often be heard several yards away. You may be able to hear a borer in a dead tree in the forest if the busy insect happens to be working as you go by.

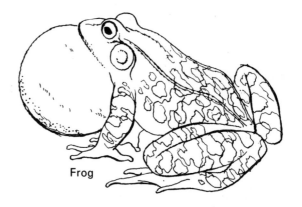

Frog

Amphibians sing with their mouths closed

Amphibians are creatures that live at least part of their lives in water. This group includes the frogs, toads and salamanders. Think of almost any sound at all, and chances are that some amphibian makes it.

There are bullfrogs with a low bellow, and cricket frogs with a high chirp. Other frogs groan, whistle, snore, bark, click, wheeze or grunt. The American toad has a trilling call which sounds rather like a police whistle. The sounds of other toads vary from a ba-a-a like a sheep to a cheep like a bird.

80

Most of the singing is done by the male frog. The large circle behind
the eye of this male frog is its ear. Males have larger ears than females.

Most of the sounds made by an amphibian are caused by the passage of
air back and forth from the mouth to the lungs. As it goes, the air vibrates
vocal cords in the throat region. Usually the throat or the sides swell up
like a balloon when the creature is singing. This acts as an echo chamber to
magnify the sound. The echo chamber serves as a sounding box. So the
amphibian does not need to open its mouth to sing any more than a drum
needs to be opened up to make its noise.

The electric catfish of tropical Africa can deliver a powerful shock.

The hiccup fish

If you have ever caught a catfish, perhaps you heard it make a little grunting sound. Some eels and other fish make a sound like this, too. The sound is often made by gulping air or by vibrations of an internal air sac or swim bladder.

Few fish can match the noise made by the pirarucu, a hiccup fish, of Brazil. Taking great mouthfuls of air, it releases them in a big bubble. The result sounds like a gigantic hiccup. These fish sometimes grow to be 3·65 metres (12 feet) long, and then their hiccup can be heard nearly a kilometre away!

The loudest amphibian

The deep jug-a-rum of the bullfrog can be heard nearly a mile away on a clear night. The bullfrog, however, is one of the largest of all frogs, and may weigh as much as 454 grams (1 pound). Smaller frogs and toads in many parts of the world can be heard even farther away. Some of the tree frogs of the tropics produce an ear-splitting shriek.

Perhaps the loudest amphibian for its size is a tree-frog called the spring peeper. This tiny frog is found over the eastern half of the United States. The smallest of all frogs, the full-grown male spring peeper can sit comfortably on your thumbnail with very little hanging over. Its high-pitched note can be heard half a kilometre away under good conditions. Yet the little songster weighs only 1·9 grams ($\frac{1}{15}$ of an ounce). If a person could sing as loud in proportion, a man weighing 72 kilograms (160 pounds) could be heard 30,577 kilometres (19,000 miles) away!

Ocean noises

Almost any kind of noise you can think of is found in the ocean. For years men spoke of the silent sea. Now, with sensitive microphones, we know that the sea is really alive with sound. Even down in the depths where no light has penetrated since the seas were formed, strange whistles, buzzes, clicks, and shrieks can be heard. Perhaps it is all these different sounds which help ocean creatures to recognise their own kind and also find their prey.

One school of fish sounds like a flock of sheep. Another sounds like pieces of paper blowing around. A group of shrimps makes a noise like bacon frying. Some kinds of barnacles sound like corn popping. A moaning sound may mean a great grouper is passing. Clicks like a high-speed telegraph coupled with high-pitched squeals may tell of the approach of a school of dolphins.

Even the great whales make a number of sounds. Perhaps the reverberations from these sounds tell the whales what lies ahead. Something like this must have been the case with a sportsman who was playing a fish at the end of a long line. When a school of whales came along, the fisherman thought his line would certainly be broken. But, to his astonishment, the huge creatures came to a stop before reaching the slender line, and then dived under it!

Dolphin

83

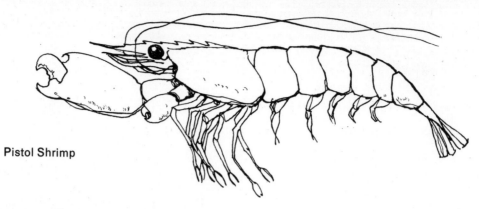

Pistol Shrimp

There really is a pistol shrimp

A scientist once captured some live shrimps and brought them into the laboratory to identify them. Putting them in a glass jar, he had hardly turned away when he heard a loud report that sounded as if the jar had cracked in half.

Then he knew what kind of shrimps he had. They were pistol shrimps. They made a noise like a shot by snapping their claws. Skin divers who swim too close to a pistol shrimp may be deafened for a while by the sudden snap of those claws.

The loudest mammal may not be the largest

The roar of a lion and the trumpeting of an elephant can be heard for many kilometres on the African plains. The splash of the great humpback whales can be heard for 16 kilometres (10 miles) or more on a calm ocean. Such large creatures, of course, would be expected to make a great deal of noise.

There is a creature that can be heard almost as far away as the loudest of the great mammals. This is the howler monkey. Living in the South American jungles, groups of these monkeys defend their territory by howling at the top of their voices. They have large lower jaws and throats which serve to amplify the sound.

When a group of these monkeys howl, the sound may be heard for several kilometres. Soon a neighbouring group howls back again. Another group joins in, and the deafening chorus may continue all over the jungle for hours.

It is hard to say which is the loudest of the more than 4,000 mammals known, but certainly the howler monkey is one of the noisiest.

84

Monkeys may be among the noisiest animals of the jungle. They squeak, scream, howl and growl. Sometimes, when they are asleep, they may even snore.

7 The structures that animals build

An animal which lives in a glass house

One of the most graceful and attractive homes is made by a deep-sea sponge that does not even look like an animal. The Venus's flower-basket is so beautiful that it seems impossible that it could have been made by a simple animal. Its woven texture is like the finest lace.

Each tiny white dot on this staghorn coral is a separate animal. A snapper fish swims by in the background.

The maker of the Venus's flower-basket is a relative of the creature that also makes the common bath sponge. The bath sponge is woven from materials in the sea by an animal which appears to be little more than a group of cells. The framework of the Venus's flower-basket is composed of the sea's commonest materials – silicon dioxide, the same material found in sand and glass. So this sponge can be said to live in a glass house which looks as if it was made of spun glass. Its home may be 90 centimetres (3 feet) long.

Corals, underwater cities built by animals

A piece of coral often appears like a plant carved in stone. Like the sponges, the hard parts of coral are a framework built of materials from the sea. Many coral animals, which look rather like tiny flowers with little moving petals, grow together and build the stony coral skeleton which serves as a home for them all.

Corals are found in a great variety of shapes and colours. Many of them have stinging cells which paralyse fish and small animals on which they feed. The most famous collection of these animals in their underwater city is the Great Barrier Reef near Australia. It is 16 to 144 kilometres (10 to 90 miles) wide and stretches for more than 1,930 kilometres (1,200 miles).

The animal which lives inside a tube

If you walk along the shore when the tide is low, you may see hundreds of pencil-sized tubes sticking out of the mud. These belong to animals known as tubeworms. Other tubeworms can be found in sand, sunken ships and the hollow spaces of coral.

Tubeworms are often very beautiful, with long feathery feelers which strain food from the sea. When they hide, however, all that can be seen is the tube, which is made by the worm itself. A substance which is secreted from its body is used to stick the sand together to form a protective covering.

The molluscs' shell serves many purposes

The clams, snails and other molluscs are soft-bodied. Without the protection of a shell they would be almost helpless, subject to attacks by enemies or tumbled about by the waves and tides. Squids and octopuses are molluscs that are strong swimmers, and thus do not need heavy shells to protect them. Many molluscs have coverings of lime which often grow into beautiful shapes and patterns. Shells are used for other purposes than protection. The common scallop swims like an underwater butterfly by flapping its shells. The female argonaut uses her shell as an egg case. Little periwinkles make their way through tight places by shouldering along with their shells. The great piddock clam uses its shell to bore a hole in the clay bank in which it lives.

Man has found other uses for shells. Oyster shells, rich in lime, are ground up and used to enrich soil. Shells have been used as ornaments, and even as money. The many interesting forms of shells are popular with collectors. One of the rarest is a shell known as the Glory of the Seas cone shell. Only about two dozen specimens are known and collectors have paid hundreds of pounds for just one shell!

Mollusc Shell

There is not really a man-eating clam

Adventure stories tell of swimmers who step between the shells of a giant clam and are held there until they drown. While this has been known to happen, the clam is not really a man-eater. It feeds on tiny organisms in the sea water. But when disturbed, it closes its shell tightly just as other clams do. Shells of such giant clams have been known to weigh over 181 kilograms (400 pounds).

Tipped up on end for a moment, the hermit crab may soon reach out
and pull its snail shell home along after it.

Open a plant gall and you are in for a surprise

Galls are strange bumps and swellings that occur on plants. If you open
one, you may find it to be the home of some little creature. It may be the
young of a wasp, fly or other insect, or it may be a tiny spider-like mite.
Each creature has its own particular gall.

When the mother insect or mite lays her eggs in the tender young part
of the plant, the part begins to swell. This swelling becomes a protective
home for the creature within.

89

An insect which builds its own log cabin

Real logs, of course, are too large for any insect to move. But twigs and little sticks are used for the house of the caddis worm. It cements them together with a glue secreted from its mouth to make a tube which just fits its body. Then it drags its strange home along over the bottom of a pond or stream.

Some caddis worms use pebbles or tiny shells for their building materials. In streams where gold is found, they have even been known to use a few little gold nuggets. Of course, to a caddis worm, gold is just the same as sand in making a home.

Caterpillars which live in tents

Not all caterpillars live in tents, but there are a few that build little homes of silk in which several hundred caterpillars may live at once.

Look for the home of the tent caterpillar in apple, peach, plum, and cherry trees. When the babies hatch out in the spring, they begin to wander in search of tender green leaves. Everywhere they go, they leave a little trail of silk secreted from glands in their mouths. When they come to a crotch of the branch on which they were hatched, they weave so many strands of silk that it soon becomes a shelter. This little silken tent keeps them safe from wind, rain and enemies.

How much silk does a silkworm make?

Probably the best-known producer of silk is the silkworm, the caterpillar of a large moth. When the silkworm is ready to change into a moth, it spins a cocoon. Within this cocoon it sheds the old caterpillar skin and forms new wings, legs, antennae and eyes.

To make silk thread, man must very carefully unwind the delicate strand of silk which has been woven into the cocoon. This thread, which is usually in one continuous piece, may be as long as 300 metres (1000 feet).

91

As the tent caterpillars walk on the outside of their home, their silk threads make it larger and larger.

The use of silk by other insects

A great many caterpillars of moths and butterflies can manufacture silk, as can the young of many bees, ants, wasps and a few other insects.

Often the silk is used for making a home or a cocoon for the young insect as it turns into an adult. Some caddis worms build silk nets in the water to help them catch food. Caterpillars will often lower themselves from one branch to another on a strand of silk.

The leaf-tying ant has one of the strangest uses for silk. Although the adults cannot produce this material, the young grubs have well-developed silk glands. So the adult ants get the grubs to help them build the nest. Taking a grub between her jaws, an ant will weave it back and forth between the edges of a curled leaf. Like a woman using a needle and thread, she sews the leaf together.

Ant hills – their size and inhabitants

The size of an ant hill depends on the kind of ant building it. Some ants do not build any homes at all. Carpenter ants make tunnels and caves in the wood of dead trees or in the lumber of buildings. Their home is entirely hidden beneath the surface.

Many mound-building ants make homes which are regular cities. Their homes may be taller than a man and measure several kilometres across. Beneath the surface are many rooms. The soil which makes the mound is brought from under the ground by the ants as they dig their tunnels. Some ants even grow mushrooms in little underground gardens.

The army ants make a home with their own bodies. These ferocious ants march through the forest, devouring every living animal in their path. When they pause to rest, they cluster together in a ball. Then, when they move on again, there is hardly a trace of their home.

Each sand grain in an anthill was brought up from below by an ant as it helped hollow out its underground home.

Social insects make the largest homes

Huge homes are often made by the so-called social insects – the ants, bees, wasps and termites that live together in large groups. Some wasp nests are several feet high, and may contain hundreds of thousands of these fiery insects. Wild bees may occupy much of the inside of a hollow tree.

The largest homes for the size of the inhabitants are probably those of certain termites. These small insects often look like white wingless ants. They feed on wood, often mixing it into the walls of their homes along with sand and clay, making walls so hard that they cannot be broken without an axe.

The mounds of tropical termites may rise to a height of 3 or $3\frac{1}{2}$ metres (10 or 12 feet) above the ground. They look like strange pointed stumps scattered over the tropical plains. Sometimes the mounds are flattened, with the edges facing north and south. This keeps them from catching the full force of the mid-day heat when the sun is in the south. Such termites are sometimes called compass termites. Several million termites may live in these homes.

The first paper makers

The people of ancient Egypt wrote on papyrus, a sort of paper which was made from the crushed stem of the papyrus plant. But in actual fact the first paper had been made a very long time before that. Hornets and wasps had been making paper millions of years before the time of the Egyptians.

To make paper, these insects chew up tiny pieces of wood. Mixing them with the saliva from their mouths, they spread the mixture out in a thin sheet. The sheet dries into a stiff dry paper.

The first pottery makers

The ancient Egyptians also knew about making pottery, but so did the wasps. The mud dauber wasps build little tubes of mud against the wall of a house or the side of a cliff. When the sun dries the mud, it becomes a hard little castle in which the young wasps can develop.

Pottery wasps actually make little jugs. Some of them are about the size of a marble. These jugs can sometimes be seen in bushes in city parks. They will have a little mud cork, too.

A wasp brings food to the young in their paper nest.

The first weavers

Although wasps and their relatives have been making paper and pottery for more than 100 million years, the first weavers and spinners were at work long before this. We can still see them at work today, for these weavers are the spiders. Their ancestors appeared on the earth nearly 400 million years ago.

The spider web and how it is used

A spider spins its web by means of little spinnerets at the end of its body. Some webs are delicate and beautiful, while others are like large flat sheets on the grass.

There are many uses for spider webs. Sometimes a spider will let out a long strand of silk until the wind catches it and carries the spider away to a new home. Jumping spiders use a strand of silk as a lifeline similar to the way a mountain climber uses his rope.

The trap-door spider lines its hole in the ground with web and makes a plug of earth and silk to close it. Garden spiders build large webs right across a path or opening between two clumps of grass. This web serves as a net to catch insects.

This fish builds its nest of bubbles

A nest made of bubbles may seem like a pretty flimsy structure, but this is not the case when made by members of the gourami family of fishes. To make their bubble nest, they blow the bubbles with their mouths, mixing them with a sticky saliva. The bubbles stick together and float to the surface of the water. There they make a raft which serves as a cradle for the eggs.

Gouramis are shaped rather like goldfish. They are popular with tropical fish collectors. If kept in a large enough aquarium, the gouramis may make a nest of their own. The Siamese fighting fish, or betta, also makes a bubble nest.

Bass

Some fish sweep the bottom of their pond

If you go slowly along in a boat over shallow water which contains bass or sunfish, you may find these fish at home above a circle of gravel on the muddy bottom. They sweep the mud away with their fins and tails until only a patch of clean gravel is left. Then, when the female lays her eggs, the male fish helps to keep them free of mud by waving his fins over them. If mud were allowed to collect on the eggs, the baby fish run the risk of suffocating.

Weaverbirds build communal houses

Each bird builds its own kind of nest. The hanging nest of the Baltimore oriole sways out at the end of a few twigs on a tall tree. The osprey, or fish hawk, makes a great nest of twigs on top of a pole or in a dead tree. The ovenbird hides her nest in the woods beneath leaves and sticks on the ground. Bluebirds nest in holes, and nighthawks nest on flat roofs of buildings right in the middle of a city.

Most of these nests are occupied by only one pair of birds; any other birds are quickly chased away. But the weaverbirds of Africa and parts of Asia build nests that are shared with others of the same species. Weaving bits of straw and reeds together, they often make huge structures containing hundreds of nests.

When they make the nest, the weaverbirds often help each other. One bird may get inside while another stays on the outside. Then they pass a reed back and forth from one to the other, sewing the nest together. The finished structure, which may contain as many as a thousand nests, looks like a huge jug or umbrella.

98

Bowerbirds build playhouses

When the early explorers visited New Guinea and Australia, they found strange little houses made of grass and twigs in the middle of tiny clearings in the forest. At first they thought that these were the playhouses of children. They soon noticed, however, that there were often birds about as big as robins carrying bright shells, shiny stones and pretty flowers to these houses.

Finally the explorers discovered how these little houses were made. They were the work of those small birds. They looked like little garden houses, or bowers, and thus the birds became known as bower-birds.

The male bowerbird makes its garden house to attract the female. He finds the brightest shells and the freshest flowers as offerings, and he entertains her there with a little dance. She usually builds the actual nest some distance away. Some bowers may be several feet across and built like little grass huts. No wonder the explorers thought they were the playhouses of children!

The female bowerbird makes a nest by herself and does not use the little bowers built by the male.

Some beaver houses may be 2·5 metres (8 feet) high, with room enough inside for a human being to stand.

The engineer in a fur coat

Probably the greatest living engineer among the wild mammals is the common beaver. It builds dams which may be more than 4 metres (15 feet) high. Some dams have been known to be as much as half a kilometre long. Most dams start out small, but are made larger as the beaver pond gets bigger.

The beaver builds dams in order to provide ponds on which to float the branches it cuts from trees with its sharp teeth. At first it cuts the trees near

100

the water. Then, as it goes farther away, it builds other ponds with canals between them. Then it can float the wood on which it feeds from as far as quarter of a kilometre away. Sometimes it makes as many as twenty canals, all going to the big pond.

The fur of the beaver has been sought by trappers for many years. Trappers pushed westward across North America, opening the land for settlers who followed them. So this peaceful and industrious rodent not only builds ponds and cuts huge trees, but the men who trapped it were largely responsible for engineering the exploration of the North American continent.

The little farmer is a pika

The pika looks like a guinea pig or a small short-eared rabbit. It lives on the slopes of high mountains in central Asia and the Himalayas and in the Rocky Mountains of North America.

During the summer, the pika eats grass and leaves and other vegetation. It also cuts grass in a small circle near its underground nest. It then spreads the grass out in the sun where it dries into hay. The pika stores the hay in piles beneath overhanging rocks.

The haystacks of the little farmer may sometimes be two or three feet tall. With these piles of hay near its warm nest, the pika has plenty of food for a winter in the mountains.

Pika

Brock the badger steals out at night to search for food.

The house-proud badger

The badger is a burrowing animal and usually builds its home in a sheltered part of a wood or an old quarry. The earth, or sett, as it is called, has a single main entrance but may consist of a series of passages which leads to various other escape routes and exits. Several burrows are sometimes joined together in this way.

The badger is a tireless animal with very powerful front feet which it uses for digging. It does not see or hear very well but has a highly developed sense of smell. The badger is a very clean creature and will not foul its sett, which is cleaned out regularly. One of the most treasured sights for the naturalist is to catch a glimpse of a badger returning to its sett with fresh bundles of grass and bracken to replace its old bedding.

Despite the fact that they will eat practically anything and do not depend on any one source of food, badgers are declining in many parts of the world. They only manage to survive by remaining hidden in daytime, venturing out at night with great caution.

102

8 Migration: facts and educated guesses

The mystery of bird migration

The migration of birds has interested man for thousands of years. Some people think they migrate because the weather becomes too cold. Others think migration may be the result of some sort of memory left over from the Ice Age, when the great glaciers forced many living creatures to move south. Still others say birds migrate because they have run out of food. But, there are many birds that remain in the same place through the bitterest winter weather. Why don't they migrate, too? Nobody can answer this question with any certainty. Food at any rate can hardly be the only reason, for most of the birds begin to head south when there is plenty of food available. The North American bobolink, for instance, may leave a sunny hayfield and its fruit, seeds and insects as early as late July.

The truth is that nobody knows exactly why birds migrate. There are a great many theories, but the real reason still remains one of nature's mysteries.

How migrating birds find their way

This is another mystery. Some scientists say they follow the rays of the sun, but many birds migrate at night. Other scientists believe they can find their way by means of the stars and constellations in the evening sky. However, birds may fly long distances on cloudy days and nights.

Do they follow the lines of the earth's magnetic force, using some kind of built-in compass? This is what many scientists believe.

All of these, however, are just theories. Birds are so good at migrating that a young bird will make its way to its winter home if neither of its parents is there to show the way. But exactly how it knows what route to follow is still unknown.

Downhill migration

There are many birds that migrate without actually going south. They move from the higher regions in summer to the protected valleys and seacoasts in winter. This is known as downhill, or vertical, migration. In the lower regions the birds can find food and shelter until spring comes once more. Then they go back to their summer homes in the higher country.

In the summer in some mountain regions of the world, crows fly over the fields. They may raise their young in tall evergreen trees of the forests. With the coming of winter, they may follow the rivers down to large lakes and to the seashore. There they stay until spring. They feed along the edge of the water and find food in abandoned cornfields of the flat land in valleys. And they may only be a few miles away from their summer homes.

Birds often migrate at night

People sometimes think that birds in their migratory flight take to the air and do not land until they reach their destination – a great journey that is practically nonstop. Many birds take weeks to migrate. During the day they feed and rest. Then, when the sun has set, they take to the air. By flying at night, birds have time to feed during the day. They can also escape many enemies.

This is not true. Bird migration is not always flight or moving up and down mountains. Some birds swim.

The greatest migration by a swimming bird

Perhaps the longest migration ever made by a flightless bird was taken by the great auk, an animal that is extinct today. This bird was about the size of a goose. It looked much like a penguin, but lived on some of the islands of the Arctic Ocean. Here it raised its single young. Then, with the coming of autumn, the great auk began to swim southward.

The emu – one of the largest flightless birds.

Great Auk

It made its way as far south as Florida – a swim of about 3,218 kilometres (2,000 miles).

Great auks lived in Newfoundland and on other northern islands until as late as the 1800s. Men killed them for their skins, which were made into warm winter garments, and for their eggs. Today there is not a single great auk left in the world.

The penguin is a flightless bird that does migrate

Some flightless birds, such as the ostrich and the emu, do not ever go far from the place where they were born. But many penguins, despite living much of their lives in water, do migrate to lay their eggs. One of the strangest journeys is that of the emperor penguins. Turning their backs on the water where they have dived and chased after fish, the emperor penguins make their way inland.

Much of the land of the frozen antarctic is covered with snow and ice, so their expert knowledge of swimming is of little help. They waddle along where the ice is rough, climbing up little hills and sliding down the other side. Where they can, they just slide along on their stomachs, rowing themselves across the ice with their flipper-like wings and steering with their feet.

106

Finally they come to the spot where they were hatched. This may be 80 kilometres (50 miles) or more from the sea. There the female lays a single egg. The male places it on his feet and settles down over it to keep it warm. Then the female slides and waddles back to the sea. Here she catches fish for a month or more. When she is fat and stuffed with extra fish for her baby, she makes her way back to her mate.

By then the little penguin is just hatching. She regurgitates the extra food she has saved for it. At this time, her mate pushes his way back to the ocean for food. He has not eaten a thing for nearly three months. When he is filled, he hurries back to his mate and their one child. Now it is her turn to go to the sea again.

They do this several times. Finally, when the baby is large enough, it accompanies its parents to the sea.

These penguins may have had to walk many days for their first swim, as they were probably hatched far inland.

Scientists speculate on the V-formation of flying geese

Usually the leader of a flock of geese is an old gander who has made the journey many times before. Behind him, in long lines like the two halves of a V, there may be as many as a hundred more. Sometimes the formation breaks up into smaller groups, or may turn into one long line streaming out diagonally behind the leader.

Perhaps the geese fly in this way because each goose thus cuts the air a little bit for the one behind it. At least this is what many scientists feel to be the reason.

Some migrating birds stay close to home while others span continents

Some Canada geese may fly all the way from the Gulf of Mexico to the arctic marshlands where they raise their young. Other geese may go no more than a few kilometres from a coastal swamp to a pond a short distance inland. Many other migrating birds show the same variety in their movements.

Some birds travel great distances each year. In Europe most long-distance migratory birds nest in northern parts of the continent and winter in tropical Africa. Many summer visitors in the northern United States spend the winter in the southern states or in Central America. The common barn swallow may build its mud nest in the northern United States and Canada and pass its winter in Brazil. The tiny humming-bird may travel from the Canadian border to Central America.

The golden plover travels even farther – with a large part of its route over water. This bird, about the size of a robin, builds its nest on far-northern arctic islands. After nesting, it flies to Nova Scotia and the eastern coast of Canada. Then it launches out over the Atlantic Ocean – some 3,861 kilometres (2,400 miles) non-stop to South America. A western branch of the golden plover family nests in northern Alaska and flies 3,218 kilometres (2,000 miles) south over open ocean to Hawaii and other Pacific islands.

Hundreds of Canada geese over the Jack Miner Migratory Bird
Foundation, Kingsville, Ontario.

Tern

The world's most travelled animal

The champion traveller of all is the arctic tern. This graceful white bird with the black cap is sometimes seen along the seacoast of New England and eastern Canada. It is more common farther north in Greenland and along arctic shores. There it makes its nest.

The arctic tern remains in the northland for only about two months. Almost as soon as the young can fly, it takes them off on a fantastic journey. From the arctic regions, the terns cross the Atlantic Ocean to the western coast of Africa. Some of them continue on down the African coast, while others cross the Atlantic Ocean again, heading for South America. Still going south, they finally reach the coast of Antarctica. There they spend a few weeks of winter. But they cannot stay too long, for they soon must head north again.

Since these birds spend their summers in both the Arctic and the Antarctic when the hours of daylight are longest, they see more total daylight than any other living creature. Their summer and winter homes are 17,699 kilometres (11,000 miles) apart. To reach them along their zigzag route, they must travel about 40,225 kilometres (25,000 miles) each year!

The migratory mammals

A number of mammals make migrations each year. The elk of the region around Yellowstone National Park in the United States move from the mountain regions to the protected valleys. Caribou wander over the arctic tundra in summer, but move to the edges of forest areas in search of better feeding in the winter.

110

Their trips may cover hundreds of kilometres, for they are the biggest wanderers of the deer family.

Bear and moose migrate from the mountain regions to the valleys, too. Even the little mole has its own way of migrating, following the earthworms on which it feeds. As the worms go down beneath the frost level, the mole tunnels right down with them. The distance between its summer and winter homes may be only 121 to 152 centimetres (4 to 5 feet) down through the soil.

Much of the common mole's life is taken up with its search for food.

Lemmings

The dangerous journey of the lemming

Perhaps the most famous migration is that of the collared lemmings of the arctic tundra. These little creatures, looking like large tail-less mice, may live a very short distance from the place where their parents and grand-parents were born. Then, suddenly, a strange urge seems to overtake most of them at once. Leaving their birthplace behind, they start out on a trip across the frozen tundra.

As they go, they are joined by other lemmings. Still more come along until there are thousands of the little animals, all running in one direction. When they come to a stream, they jump right in and swim across. They

112

climb over bits of moss and tumble down off the rocks. Many of the lemmings are killed as they run along, for hawks, ravens and gulls attack them from the air. Foxes and weasels pounce on them, too.

If their direction of travel takes them to the edge of the sea, the lemmings jump right in. They swim until they are exhausted. Soon their journey is ended, and only a few of the animals remain on the tundra to keep the species alive.

Why do lemmings undertake this strange migration? Nobody can answer the question with certainty. However, as a female lemming may produce several litters in the year, a shortage of food may start the little animals searching for a new place to live. And for a long time it was a mystery as to why they plunge into the sea. At last scientists think they know the answer. The sea may seem just like another stream to the lemmings, and since they have been able to swim others, they jump into the sea, too.

The menace of the red tide

Not all migratory creatures are large animals or birds. There are a number of migratory animals found in the ocean where it may be easy to go from place to place.

One of the most dreaded migrations is that of the red tide, which occurs on the coast of Florida. It is caused by the sudden appearance of billions of one-celled creatures known as dinoflagellates. Their bodies are found in such immense numbers that they colour the sea water. Fish and other marine animals which come in contact with them soon die and are cast up on the beach in great numbers.

Actually, the red tide is not so much a migration as it is a population explosion. For months and even years, the dinoflagellates get along in normal numbers without any great effect on their neighbours. Then, for some unknown reason, they suddenly increase. Poison produced by their bodies kills millions of fish, causing fishermen to put away their nets. Bathing beaches must close until ocean currents change and sweep the red tide out to sea.

Causes of the false bottom in the ocean

Today, many fishing boats and ocean-going ships have a device known as a depth-finder. A depth-finder acts on the principle that a signal sent to the bottom of the ocean will come back as an echo. The echo is recorded by a special instrument. The longer the echo takes to return, the farther away the bottom.

It was not long after the invention of this device that ships began to report a false bottom – an echo from something near the surface. At night the false bottom might be a few fathoms beneath the boat, but during the day it was far deeper.

Finally it was discovered what the false bottom might be. Tiny floating organisms known as plankton drift up near the surface of the water at night. During the day they drop down below the penetration of the sun's rays. While plankton organisms are too small to produce an echo, the millions of little fish, squid and other creatures which feed on them are large enough to affect ships' instruments. So the ocean has its vertical migrations, just as on land.

To catch certain fish, follow their migration pattern

Not only do fish migrate, but their travels are of great importance to fishermen. For example, fishermen have been known to catch different fish each month of the year – all in the same place. As the flounders go past one fisherman's home along the Virginia shore in summer, he scoops them up with a bottom net known as a trawl. Bluefish are caught later, in another kind of net, and marlin and tuna are caught on hook and line. Later he uses special lines to catch drum, bass and sturgeon. When the mackerel appear in late winter, he catches them in gill nets.

Some fish migrate because of changing water temperature. Others follow the plankton or other food as it drifts along on ocean currents. Still others lay their eggs at one point and spend the rest of their lives many miles away. And, of course, there are many fish whose reason for migrating we have not yet discovered.

114

A blue marlin leaps high in the air.

Some of these salmon may weigh 18 kilograms (40 pounds or more as they fight their way up an Alaska stream.

The salmon run is a race against all odds

There are two main species of salmon, the Atlantic salmon, which migrates between the Atlantic ocean and European coasts and rivers, and the Pacific salmon which lives in north Pacific waters and visits rivers on the Pacific coasts of America and Asia. Salmon spend several years in the ocean before returning to the place where they lay their eggs.

No matter where the salmon has been, it somehow finds the very river in which it was spawned. Tests with tagged baby salmon show that they

116

drift down to the sea from their birthplace, disappear somewhere in the ocean – and come back to the same river to lay their eggs.

Thousands of salmon may crowd into a bay during a salmon run. They may be packed so closely that they bump the bottoms of boats. Here they are easily taken in nets. As they swim up the rivers, they are attacked by birds and mammals which come to share the feast. Along the wilder streams, bears, wildcats and cougars wade into the water and catch them.

So intent on their purpose are the salmon that many of them do not eat during the time they fight their way upriver. In fact, they may never eat again, for many die soon after laying their eggs.

A fish that travels across land

Although the eel looks more like a snake, it is really a long slender fish. Its life story is just the opposite of that of the salmon, for eels spawn in the ocean. After the eggs have hatched, the transparent young make their way back to the rivers. Swimming upstream, they enter lakes and ponds. Remaining in fresh water until they are ready to spawn, the eels may grow to a length of 1·52 metres (5 feet). Then they begin the journey back to the sea to lay their eggs.

If an eel comes to a dam in the river, it may wait for a rainy night to leave the water. It may then wriggle over the damp ground until it comes to the river again to continue its journey. It may go thousands of kilometres until it reaches the spot where it was born – the deep water near Bermuda.

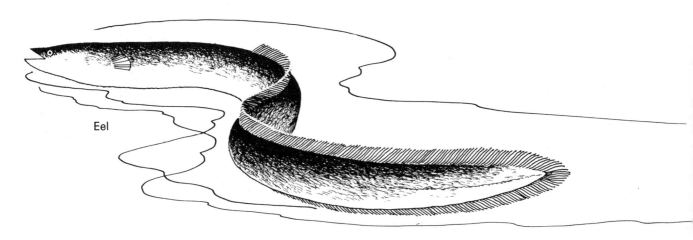

Eel

Sea turtles must risk the dangers of land to reproduce

Every year, the female sea turtles arrive at the beaches of certain islands. Each turtle awkwardly crawls inland by means of her flippers. Then she digs a hole in the sand. She lays her eggs in the hole, covers them and crawls back to the water. The turtle's ocean journeys may then take her hundreds of kilometres away but the next year she returns to the same beach.

In a few weeks the baby turtles hatch out of the eggs. Hastening to the sea as fast as their little flippers will carry them, they are at the mercy of gulls and other creatures which gobble them up by the hundreds. Out of thousands of baby turtles, only a dozen or so may escape.

Why do sea turtles insist on living such a perilous life? The answer is simply that they have no other choice. Sea turtles are reptiles. The eggs of reptiles must be laid on land. So the turtle is forced to expose herself and her babies to all the dangers of land even though she is a creature of the sea.

This turtle digs a hole in the sand to bury her eggs.

Other migrations in the sea

Actually, there are thousands of sea migrations. Some creatures, like floating jellyfish, may drift with the ocean currents. Horseshoe crabs come up on land to lay their eggs, following the more than 300-million-year-old pattern of their ancestors. Their egg-laying journey to the beach from a short distance offshore has been called the earth's oldest beach party.

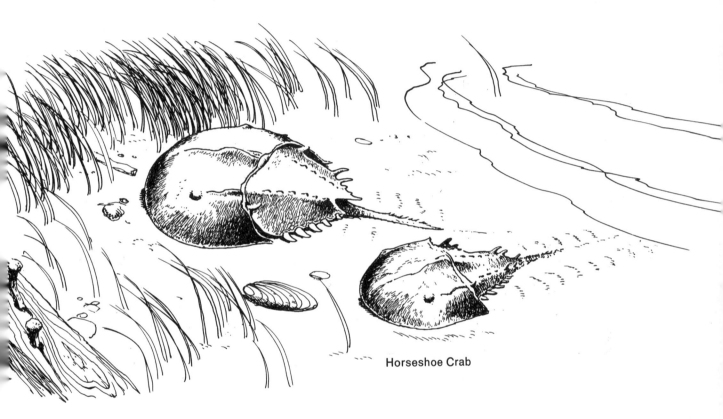
Horseshoe Crab

Great blue whales may swim in northern seas and have their calves in the waters near the South Pole. Palolo worms in the South Pacific Ocean near the Fiji Islands come swarming to the surface each autumn, produce their eggs and disappear for another year. Scallops move in and out of the mouths of rivers. Shrimps, prawns, lobsters and other crustaceans wander from place to place according to the season. And fish by the millions migrate from one part of the sea to another, sometimes changing the shade of the water by their great numbers.

Some startling theories about the migration of fur seals

The chilly Pribilof Islands off the coast of Alaska are the home of some of the most famous seals on earth. These are the fur seals, which visit the islands by the thousands each spring. No more than a certain number of seals are allowed to be killed each year. This is a wise conservation measure. The rest of the seals soon enter the water again and start on their long migration.

No ship has followed the fur seals during their travels. Probably they go far south, down to southern Pacific waters. In fact it is thought by some scientists that they may travel as far as 9,000 kilometres (about 6,000 miles).

Occasionally a fur seal found far out at sea has been killed for scientific purposes. When scientists study its stomach contents to find out more about its life, they sometimes discover an interesting fact. Its stomach may contain fish which are normally found far beneath the surface of the ocean.

So the fur seal may be not only a champion distance swimmer, but it may be a champion diver as well. Until more is known about this interesting animal, however, much of its life remains a mystery.

The hiding places of the frog

One of the common sounds of spring is the song of the frogs and toads in the swamps. Some of these frogs just make their way up from the mud where they have been buried all winter. But many toads, spring peepers and tree frogs have farther to travel. They have been hidden beneath decaying leaves or under old logs and must leave their forests and fields to make the journey back to the swamp. Sometimes they can be heard singing on a warm spring evening before they have yet reached the water. When they finally get to the swamp, they mate and lay their eggs.

120

Fur seals on St Paul Island, in the Pribilof Group off Alaska. The
route of their sea migration is still one of nature's mysteries.

Look to their ancestry for the reason amphibians lay their eggs in water

In the earlier days of the earth there were no animals living on land. For
millions of years the only backboned animals were the fish. Scientists
think that one of them finally developed lungs and the ability to walk on
dry earth. This was the first land-dwelling vertebrate animal. Its descen-
dants became the first amphibians. From these early beginnings came the
higher vertebrates – reptiles, birds and mammals.

These higher creatures can live and have their young on dry land, but
amphibians have remained dependent on moisture. Their eggs would
quickly die out of water. Each year they return to lay their eggs – just as
their ancestors probably did more than 350 million years ago.

121

Butterfly Town and the story of its inhabitants

There are few, true migratory insects. Many insects lay their eggs and die before winter. Others hide beneath a bit of bark, or burrow down into the soil. A few of the butterflies, however, actually go south for the winter. Most famous of these is the monarch, or milkweed, butterfly. As the days of summer draw to a close, the monarch butterfly heads south like the birds. Some merely go a short distance to the warmth of a sheltered valley, others fly across lakes and rivers, towns and cities and spend the winter far to the south of their summer home.

The greatest gathering of butterflies in winter is so large that an entire city has come to be known as the Butterfly Town. This town is Pacific Grove, California. Each autumn the monarch butterflies come by the hundreds of thousands – some from as far away as Alaska or British Columbia. There are so many of them that entire trees turn orange and black with the colour of their wings. Such numbers of tourists come to see them that the town has had to pass special laws protecting the colourful insects.

The butterflies spend the winter among the trees of Pacific Grove, remaining quiet for days at a time. In the spring they begin to head north. Usually they do not get very far. Their strength has been used up during the long winter. When they find a suitable milkweed plant they may lay their eggs, flutter a bit further, and die.

The young caterpillars soon hatch out. In about a month's time they have turned into adult butterflies. Then they continue the journey started by their parents. With no knowledge of the route they must travel, they make their way farther north. Sometimes the trip is too long for them as well. So they in turn lay their eggs and leave the rest of the journey to their children.

Finally the children or the grandchildren of the Pacific Grove butterflies reach their summer home. But autumn is fast approaching. So they soon turn to the south, as their ancestors did before them. Guided by some strange sense, they find their way to a spot they have never seen. Then Pacific Grove, California, welcomes the butterflies once again.

122

This monarch butterfly, photographed in Vermont, may spend its winter many hundreds of kilometres to the south.

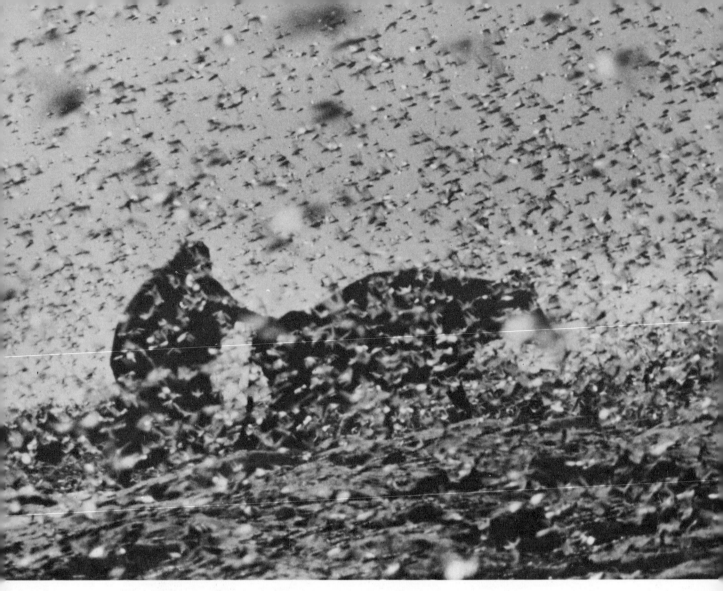

One of the most dreaded migrations – a swarm of flying locusts. Here
they almost hide a farmer and his ox as they plough a field.

The dreaded insect migrant and a sometime welcome visitor

Many of the scale insects do not move more than a few millimetres all
their adult lives. They remain in the same spot, sucking the sap from the
stem of a plant.

Other insects, however, travel great distances. Plagues of locusts sweep
over the fields of the Near East. They devour everything in their path and
darken the sun's rays with their numbers. Thousands of army worms
have been known to march through a field of oats, chewing on the leaves
of the plants and leaving nothing but the stems.

The army ants which travel through the jungle never seem to have a permanent home. They merely go from one spot to another, eating every living creature they can catch. Even an elephant stands aside to let them pass. But when the ants come to a jungle village they may actually be welcomed. The people leave the house while the ants explore every room. When the ferocious insects finally leave, there is not a cockroach or mouse left in the house.

A group of army ants in the Panama Canal Zone. The army ants of Africa are also known as driver ants.

9 Age limits in animals

Do not measure size when you want to know an animal's age

Have you ever watched a mother bird feeding her young just after they have learned to fly? She looks so small and busy compared to them as they sit around her on a tree limb or follow her along the ground. Their fluffy new feathers make them appear larger than she is. They may be so well fed and fat that they weigh more, too. Only after they have been out on their own for a time do they seem to shrink to normal size.

The young of other animals may be larger and heavier than their parents too. So it is hard to guess an animal's age by its size. Just because it is large does not mean it is old. And since animals do not usually get grey hair or show any wrinkles, it is not easy to find out their age even by looking closely.

The scientists' way to determine the age of animals

In order to determine just how old an animal may be, scientists have to look closely at such things as teeth, beaks, horns, scales, feet and even bones. Of course, the animal must be caught for such close study, and this is not always an easy task. Special traps can catch mice without hurting them, but how can you make a moose stand still long enough to count its teeth?

Constant danger threatens the life of animals

Almost anything may cut short the life of an animal. There are many dangers constantly facing a living creature. Few animals live as long in the wild as in captivity.

126

A woodpecker feeds her young. When the youngster is ready to fly, it may almost sparkle in contrast to its work-worn parent.

Nearly every animal must always be alert for enemies. If you watch some birds feeding, you will see that they seldom take more than a bite or two without looking around for danger. A rabbit that becomes too interested in a patch of clover might not notice the weasel sneaking up on it. The weasel, in turn, might be so intent on the rabbit that it does not see the fox. And even though the fox has few natural enemies, it still has to be forever on the watch for dogs, hunters and traps.

Other things besides enemies may shorten the life of an animal. Baby birds get chilled in the nest while the parents are away finding food. Fleas and mites may rob an animal of much of its fur so that it cannot stand the winter cold. Diseases can wipe out an entire population. And if animals are lucky enough to escape these hazards, their numbers may build up so fast that they can run out of food. So a wild animal which lives to a ripe old age is lucky indeed.

128

Many large animals do live longer than smaller ones

If you compare the life span of a large animal with that of a small one, you may find that the larger one lives longer. This is not always true, for there are a number of exceptions.

Horses are large animals, but only a few have reached the age of fifty. On the other hand, owls have been known to reach sixty years of age. And man, halfway between the owl and the horse in size, may live to be more than a hundred years of age. It does not always follow, therefore, that large size and long life go together.

Among the tiny mammals are many which live their lives in but a few short months. A mouse faces many dangers, but even if his enemies do not catch him, the little creature may live scarcely more than a year or two. Perhaps raising families cuts its life short – a female mouse may have her first babies when she is only four months old. And she may produce as many as six litters of young each year.

To our knowledge whales do not live to be centuries old

If many large animals live longer than their smaller neighbours, wouldn't a whale live for centuries? The actual fact is that we do not know.

To be sure just how long a whale may live, a record would have to be kept of the date of its birth. Then there would have to be some way to keep track of it until it dies. This would be a tremendous task.

Even though we do not know the age to which a whale may live, careful studies by biologists show that they probably do not live for centuries as was once believed. Many scientists say they probably live about a hundred years.

The oldest whale about which there seems to be a record was a killer whale known as Old Tom. His appearance apparently could not be mistaken for any of the others in his pack. Old Tom was said to have swum around an Australian port for more than eighty years.

The exact age of the great whales may remain one of the secrets of the seas for years to come.

That an elephant can live for a hundred years is debatable

The age of an elephant in the wild is hard to determine. Many elephants live their entire lives away from the prying eyes of man. It is impossible to tell just how old they may become.

In spite of its venerable appearance, the elephant probably does not live as long as many people believe. There are many stories about elephants living far longer than human beings, but the longest one known to have lived with certainty was sixty-nine years. This creature, a female named Jessie, was an Indian elephant which lived in the zoo at Sydney, Australia.

The life-span of people

It is hard even to tell just how long the oldest person may have lived. Birth certificates were not always filled out in earlier days. When people move, their family records may be lost. And as a person becomes old, his memory may fail him. With few people still alive to remember exactly when he was born, a person may have a hard time telling his own age.

Among people who seem to have good records as to their age there are several who have lived at least 105 years. A woman by the name of Catherine Raymond lived 107 years. A Canadian, Pierre Joubert, born in 1701, lived about 113 years.

Beyond these ages, however, one begins to wonder how accurate the records may be. Many of the stories of great age date back to centuries ago. In Scandinavia, for instance, a man by the name of Drakenberg who died in 1772 is supposed to have lived for 146 years.

Perhaps the longest life of all, if the records can be believed, which is doubtful, is that of Thomas Parr in England. His death is recorded in 1635 at the supposed age of 152.

Tortoises may hold the record for long life

If you have ever seen a giant Galapagos tortoise you can understand why people think these great creatures must live to a tremendous age. Their

This Galapagos tortoise may be 150 years old. Feeding on leaves and fruit, it cuts neat bite-size chunks with its toothless jaws.

wrinkled skins and slow movements make them look ancient.

Some of these tortoises may actually live a hundred or even 150 years, but it is hard to keep accurate records for so long. If this is the case, the tortoises may hold the record for long life among animals.

Tortoises walk on land, while the true turtles swim in the sea. It is hard to discover the age of a sea turtle, as it is out in the open ocean much of its life. But scientists feel the turtles may live about as long as the tortoises – if a giant shark does not get them first!

Bands and ear tags can help tell an animal's age

Leg bands and ear tags are numbered bits of plastic or metal which can be attached to birds and other animals. Then, if the animal is ever found again, the number on the tag tells where and when it was originally banded. If a scientist finds an animal with a tag put on ten years before at a spot a thousand kilometres away, he knows the animal is at least ten years old and has travelled a thousand kilometres. Leg bands have given us much of our knowledge of the migration and age of birds.

One possible way in which scientists may be able to find out about the age of a whale is to tag a baby whale soon after birth and hope it will keep the tag throughout its life. A plastic disc, perhaps, could be attached harmlessly to one of its fins. Then, if the whale is caught years later, the date on the disc would tell how long it has lived.

It would not be easy to tag a whale, even if it was a six-metre (twenty-foot) infant. The mother whale would try to protect her baby, and the whole flock, or pod, of whales might help her.

What you should do if you find a banded bird

Thousands of harmless bands are placed on the legs of birds each year. If you ever find a dead bird with one of these bands on its legs you should carefully save the band, for it may be useful to someone who is keeping a record of bird movements.

As the years go by, the records from bird bands, the ear tags of mammals, and the fin tags of fish will be more valuable. They will tell much about the age and habits of animals. Since thousands of animals may be tagged for each one that is ever found again, it takes a great deal of time to learn all we want about them.

The life-span of birds

Although leg bands can tell about the age of birds, the study takes many years. In the meantime, we have only a few records to help us know how long they live.

132

Many small birds survive through a few winters, but probably do not live more than four or five years. The larger birds may live longer. There are records of crows and geese that lived for thirty years. Pelicans and eagles have been known to live more than fifty years.

People often feel that a pet parrot may live for more than a century, but there are very few records to prove it. A parrot can live for fifty years or more, but century-old parrots seem to belong in the land of legend.

There is a good record for what was perhaps the longest-lived bird. This was an eagle owl. Cared for and carefully sheltered during its long life in captivity, it lived to be sixty-eight years old.

Jasper Miner banding a Canada goose at the Jack Miner Migratory Bird Foundation, Inc., Kingsville, Ontario.

The domestic life of the swan

One of the most familiar and best-loved birds is the swan. Its grace and beauty have inspired poets and musicians. It appears to have much more character than other birds, although it has a reputation for being unfriendly towards man. Some swans live placidly into great old age – one is known to have reached its seventieth year.

The most familiar of these birds is the mute swan with the characteristic knob on its beak. It lives in the northern hemisphere of Europe and Asia, and has in recent years been introduced into the Americas and Australia. These birds have been domesticated in Britain since before the twelfth century, and man has afforded them protection on the quiet lakes and rivers of great country houses and public parks.

Australia, of course, has its own swan, the handsome black swan, with its bright red beak and shiny black plumage.

A snowy owl with her chicks.

A picture of grace and beauty, the mute swan swims proudly by.

The captive bird lives longest

It is important to remember that it is only in captivity that accurate records of an animal's age and behaviour can be made. Animals in the wild face many natural hazards and enemies which may end their lives while they are in their prime. Birds are no exception to this rule. All the prizes for old age go to captive birds, to such species as cockatoos, geese and parrots. Several owners of ravens have also claimed the top award with life-spans for their birds of over 100 years, but none is accepted as authentic.

One species which leads a somewhat uncertain life is the snowy owl, which lives in the barren lands of the Arctic Circle. The main food of the owls is lemmings and hares – both of these animals being subject to reproductive cycles. This means that in some years very few young are successfully reared and in others the population explosion is such that thousands of animals are forced to migrate. To keep pace with these good and bad food years, the snowy owl lays a greater or lesser number of eggs. In really bad years it may not try to breed at all.

A rare old bird

That comical creature, the pelican, is not only a bird which can live for many years, it is also one of the oldest species still inhabiting the earth. The bones of its relatives have been traced back 40 million years. The large extendable pouch under its long beak can hold as much as 13 litres (3 gallons) of liquid – much more than the capacity of its stomach. So perhaps there is some truth in the old nineteenth-century American limerick which begins, 'A rare old bird is the pelican, his beak holds more than his belican'.

Many insects are orphans at birth

Looking at another side of the animal world, we find that most insects scarcely live longer than it takes to lay their eggs. As soon as the parents

In the wild, pelicans usually live in large flocks close to rivers.

mate and produce eggs, they seem to lose all interest in life. Within a few days they die. When the babies hatch out, they are on their own.

New insect babies are not helpless, however. They have some kind of wonderful knowledge of just what to do. They seem to be able to find their own food, protect themselves from enemies, and build their nests without any parents to show them how to go about it. Scientists still do not know just how an insect is able to do all these things without being taught. This strange knowledge is known as instinct.

The insects' life-span

When an insect hatches out of the egg, it may look quite different from its adult appearance. Caterpillars turn into butterflies, grubs into beetles, and maggots into flies. Young insects which look very different from their parents are known as larvae. Other insects, such as little grasshoppers, look quite like their parents and are called nymphs.

An insect larva finally turns into a pupa. A moth cocoon is a kind of pupa. After a while the pupa turns into an adult. Nymphs gradually become adults without going through a pupal stage.

Not all these stages are the same length in the life cycle of an insect. The eggs may be laid in the autumn and not hatch until spring. Then, after they hatch, the insect may become an adult in a few weeks. On the other hand, the eggs of some kinds of aphids, or plant lice, may hatch while they are still in the mother's body. Thus she gives birth to living young. Then the aphid nymphs and adults may live for months.

Once the seventeen-year locust turns adult, it has not long to live

The periodical cicada, or seventeen-year locust, spends seventeen years beneath the ground as a nymph. It feeds on sap from the roots of plants. Then, in the late spring of its last year, it comes up out of the ground. It sheds its skin and tries out its newly formed wings. Within a very few weeks it mates, lays eggs and dies. So even though it lives a great length of time as a nymph, it may live less than a month as an adult.

The Founders' Tree – a giant California redwood. Such a tree was a forest giant at the time of Christ, and has been growing ever since.

Animals must yield to plants when it comes to age

We have to look away from the animal world, into the world of plants to find the oldest known living thing on earth. No animal can live as long as even a middle-aged tree.

The elms and oaks which shade a city park may be 200 years old. Where a forest has been undisturbed, the trees may be even older.

The giant redwoods of the Pacific coast regions in North America may grow to be more than 2,000 years old. Their close relatives, the sequoias, may be 3,000 years old.

There are trees, however, which are still older. These trees are the bristlecone pines of the mountains in the western United States. Some specimens in the White Mountains of California are estimated to be 4,000 years old. This means they had been living for 1,000 years when today's mighty sequoia trees were just tiny seedlings!

These creatures are sometimes called the immortals

Even though any plant or animal must finally die, there is one group of living creatures which scientists sometimes refer to as the immortals. These are the tiny one-celled organisms known as protozoans, algae and bacteria. Sometimes they are all known by one name – the protists.

One-celled creatures are among the smallest of living things. When the time comes for many of these minute bits of life to produce more of their kind, they simply split in two. Therefore each new protist is half of the original one. Soon it grows to full size and splits once again. This goes on and on.

In this way, a protist passes itself on from one generation to another, dividing in half each time. So a newly formed organism is in actual fact one half of its parent. Or to put it another way, when the parent divides, it is almost as if it becomes young all over again, for it suddenly turns into two children.

Four hundred times larger than normal size, the shell of a one-celled marine animal looks like a snail covered with fish net.

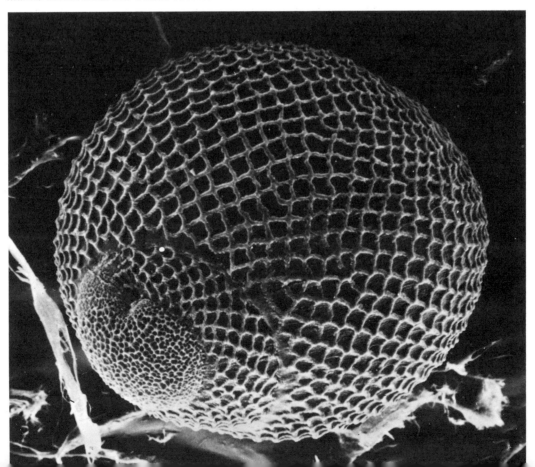

Dogs

10 Humour in animals

Intelligence enables animals to play

Stop to think of the creatures you have seen playing together. What kind of animals were they?

Chances are they were mammals or birds. You have probably never seen grasshoppers playing tag, or frogs pretending they were fighting. The reason is that it takes a certain amount of intelligence to play. An animal has to be able to act in a way that it does not really mean. In other words, it has to pretend. Scientists say that only animals with higher brain powers can do this.

Some reasons for animal play

You have probably seen a kitten or a puppy chase a ball or pounce on a dry leaf. Maybe you have seen a colt run through a pasture, or a lamb springing in the air like a rubber ball. Perhaps you have wondered why these animals played so hard that they nearly crashed into a fence or tumbled in a heap. Part of the answer, at least, is that it helps to prepare the animal for living. Of course, a domestic pet may not ever have to find its own food or escape from enemies or in general fend for itself. But if it were out on its own, it might easily run into danger and its life might depend on quick action.

140

This playful kitten is developing her skills for later life.

Perhaps you have noticed that you seldom want to play when you are tired. Play helps work off extra energy. This may be one reason why young animals play more than their parents.

Because an animal seems comical to you it is not necessarily being playful

By no means are all comical animals trying to be playful. They may be funny without trying to be. And what seems funny to us may not be funny at all to the animal. It is usually just that people can see the humour in a situation. If you look hard enough you can find something humorous in almost any animal. In fact, scientists tell us that man is the only creature that actually laughs.

Comic of the sea, the hermit crab runs around as if he was forever playing hide-and-seek.

Crabs can be funny

To many people, crabs are about the sourest animals one could think of. Yet even a crab has his funny side, whether it be a hermit crab, a swimming crab, a fiddler crab, or a land crab.

The hind part of the body of hermit crabs is soft and unprotected, so they usually tuck it into a shell which once belonged to another sea dweller. Then they walk around dragging the shell behind them. When a hermit crab gets too big for its shell and cannot find another the right size, it may steal the shell from another crab. Crabs whose shells have been stolen may utilise other devices for protection.

One was seen with his tender abdomen tucked into the only thing available – a tin can. He bumped along, advertising tomato soup everywhere he went!

Swimming crabs seem to have a boundless curiosity. Since they may eat almost anything, they are forever poking into things in their search for food. Fiddler crabs are the ballet dancers of the salt marshes. The male has one huge claw which he waves back and forth. In this way he signals to the female. Fiddlers run sideways like a flash, stopping suddenly to wave that claw. They run so fast with the one big claw that it seems as if they are trying to steal it. If you frighten them, they duck into their hole in the hardened mud. Then they keep looking out at you and ducking back in, just like a game of peek-a-boo.

There are many kinds of land crabs. One type, the ghost crab, hides in a hole deep in the sand during the day, and runs about the beach at night. If you catch a ghost crab and let it go in the daytime, it will quickly bury itself in the sand. It does not hide completely, however. It is too interested in the next move of its viewer. Like most crabs, it has its eyes on stalks, and it leaves them sticking up out of the sand. If you throw some more sand on it, those eyes come poking up in a moment. If you should try covering the crab with a whole handful of sand, there is a tiny earthquake there beneath the surface – and the crab struggles and pushes itself up until its eyes appear again.

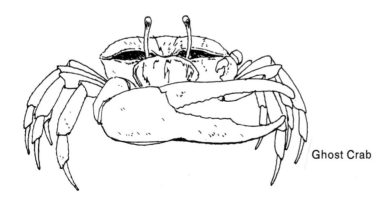

Ghost Crab

He looks bad, but he is all bluff. The harmless American puff adder, or hognose snake, puts on one of the most amazing acts.

Look for the comical snake

Plenty of people have seen comical snakes. The trouble is that many persons have been taught to be afraid of snakes. But a snake is just as much a part of our world as a snail, or a sparrow, or a spruce tree.

One of the funniest snakes is one that is most feared by many people. This is the hognose snake, or puff adder. Although it is completely harmless, it puts on an astonishing act of bluffing. Flattening itself out and taking a deep breath, it swells until it looks twice its normal size. Then it hisses and strikes as if it were going to eat you alive.

It is at this point that most people run the other way. But if you stay long enough to see what will happen next, a surprising thing takes place. Seeing that its bluff does not work, the snake goes into the second part of its act. Twisting and turning, it struggles as if it had suddenly caught some terrible disease. Then, with its mouth open, it rolls over dead.

Pick it up with a stick, and the snake hangs perfectly limp. But drop it to the earth on its stomach, and it quickly rolls over on its back. Apparently,

144

the snake seems to feel that the only position for a dead snake is upside down.

Keep turning the snake right side up, and it will keep turning itself over in the proper dead position. Finally, if you continue to do this long enough, you will see the third part of its act. The dead snake comes to life and crawls away.

Cat

Crow

Chief mischief makers among the birds

The crows, magpies and jays can be counted on to keep things lively most of the time. One pet crow enjoyed teasing a pet cat. He would wait until the cat was asleep and then quietly sneak up, steal the food out of the cat's dish, and peck the cat's tail. Crows are good mimics, too, often imitating the wails and howls of other animals.

Jays and magpies are as full of mischief as the crows. A camper at Crater Lake National Park in the United States, put his car keys down on a picnic table for a moment. A western jay saw the shiny keys, picked them up, and flew off with them to the top of a tree. It took two boys, a rope and most of the morning to get the keys back again.

Magpies, being larger than jays, can carry objects of fair size. The owner of a new petrol station which was decorated with streamers and shiny tinfoil strips could not believe his eyes one morning when he came to work. Half his tinfoil had been stolen, and two magpies were quarrelling over a long strip of red and white streamer. While he watched, they sailed off with it over the fields, still arguing. The matter was finally settled when the streamer tore in half and the magpies carried it off into the sky in two different directions.

Bird junk collectors

Nearly any bird may be a junk collector at some time or other. The nests of birds may contain all sorts of things. If a bird spies a bit of ribbon, a sweet paper or a broken balloon, it is apt to weave it right into the nest it is building. Many people put out string for birds to use, but it is important that the string be kept short. If it is more than a few inches long it may get twisted round the bird's neck or feet. A nest of one wood thrush took on a gay look when the thrush wove pink facial tissue into the nest. There it stayed, until heavy rain washed it away.

The chipping sparrow used to be called a horsehair bird, because it generally lined its nest with the long hairs which dropped from a horse's mane or tail in the spring. One chipping sparrow used a different kind of hair for her nest. She had managed to find a few horsehairs for the inner lining, but there were apparently not enough for the rest of the nest. So she filled the blank spaces in with several dozen porcupine quills – sharp points and all.

The waltzing woodcock

The woodcock is a brown bird a little larger than a robin. It has a long beak with which it pulls earthworms out of the ground. It has such a funny way of walking that people have given it all sorts of names. It has been called timber doodle, bog sucker, waddle snipe and whatzit.

Seeing a woodcock walk, you would think he was keeping time to some strange music. Stepping forward, he squats a bit, bows and teeters, sways back a little, and then takes another step. For variety, he may stamp once or twice with his feet.

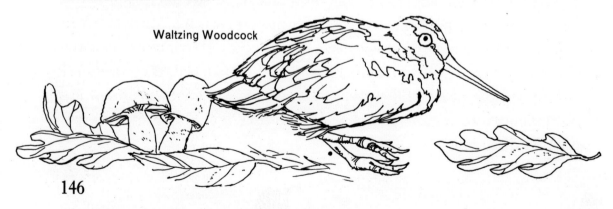
Waltzing Woodcock

Actually, the woodcock is going about the business of getting a meal. Earthworms in the soil beneath his feet sense the pressure and the motion above them and, apparently searching for gently falling rain, come up to the surface just as they do on rainy nights. The woodcock is waiting for them – doing a few extra steps just in case there should be another worm.

The comical ways of apes and monkeys

One of the most important differences between the apes and monkeys and other mammals is the possession of what is called the free hand. In all

This comical clown face belongs to a baby ape.

species the front limbs are still used for walking about but they are not essential for this purpose. Hands are free to be used for climbing and to grasp and lift things. This is one of the characteristics of apes and monkeys which bring them closer to man.

Another is the degree of their intelligence, and their ability to learn and imitate. Always restless and active, the chimpanzee is a celebrated entertainer at zoos and circuses, causing much amusement with his human antics.

Chimps have been taught to count and paint pictures, ride bicycles and do quite complicated things with their hands, such as untying knots and using keys to open locks, which need careful co-ordination between the fingers and the brain.

Many of the apes and monkeys seem to enjoy the conditions of captivity, so long as they can mix with others of their kind. Most of them are sociable and do not like to be left alone. One of the most entertaining of apes when young is the orang-utan but it tends to become very sullen and listless with age. The mighty gorilla never seems to settle happily into the confines of a zoo home and, compared with his chattering cousins the monkeys, seems to be waiting silently for an escape which he knows in his heart will never come.

The playful mermaid is really a manatee

Many animals play most when they are young. Then they settle down when they get older. The Florida manatee, on the other hand, is often just the opposite.

Manatees are sometimes called sea cows. Heavy and seal-like in appearance, they are slow-moving mammals which feed on plants in the warm shallow water. Christopher Columbus thought they were mermaids because they float upright and hold their babies just as a human mother would.

Life seems to be very serious for a manatee baby. It takes everything soberly, and seldom plays at all. Not so with its parents, however. Sometimes they start diving and chasing each other in the water. Now and

Christopher Columbus thought the manatee was a mermaid – even if it
did have a bristly moustache.

then they give a slap with those great flippers. And when nearly half a ton
of manatee goes crashing about, the playful mermaid is quite a sight. But
the baby does not enter into the fun. It remains aloof, looking on sadly at
all the foolishness, as if thinking its parents have gone crazy.

Get ready for mischief when you hear playful as a porpoise

Many members of the whale family always seem to be ready for a frolic. The smaller leaps of the porpoises and dolphins cannot equal the crashing jump of the 15 metres (50 foot) humpback whale, but these mammals are full of fun. Not only do they play around the prow of a ship as it speeds through the water, but it would appear that they like to make up games of their own.

Finding a sea turtle, the playful mammals will nudge it around like an underwater volley ball. Sometimes, if it is not too large, they may even force it to the surface and toss it in the air. The poor turtle struggles to get away, but this seems only to make the game all the better. They do not hurt it, however, and they finally let it go.

The common porpoise in marine aquariums is really the bottle-nosed dolphin. Even in captivity it seems to enjoy itself and its antics never fail to entertain.

There is a true story of a woman who leaned too far over the rail at an aquarium and spilled the entire contents of her handbag into the water. Thereupon a dolphin tossed everything straight back at her – lipstick, soggy handkerchief, pencil, money, notebook – each accompanied by a generous spray of water.

The otter, merrymaker of the wild

If the dolphin is the most playful mammal of the sea, the honours for freshwater pranks would go to the otter. It spends as much time in fun and frolic as almost any other mammal. Otters may play tag around a beaver until the poor rodent is frantic. They will toss a snake out of the water and be there to catch it when it lands.

Otters often make mud slides. Climbing up a river bank, they make it slippery with their wet bodies. By lying on their stomachs, they can slide down head first into the water. They do this again and again, even returning to the same spot months later. They slide down snow banks in the winter in the same way.

150

A playful whale leaps high out of the water. When it lands, the onlookers often get a surprise – in the form of a sudden shower.

Bird nests, rubbish bins, picnic baskets – they are all the same to the raccoon. With those clever hands and that dark mask, no wonder he is known as the playful burglar.

The playful burglar

This creature could be none other than the raccoon. With the black mask across its face, the 6 kilogram (15 pound) animal looks like a little burglar. It acts like one, too, as it steals farmers' corn and lifts lids off dustbins. It steals eggs from chicken coops and even catches goldfish in garden pools.

The little creature is so playful that it is hard to stay angry with him for very long. Everything must be explored, from a knothole in a log to the ashes of an old picnic fire. Those probing black paws are like small human hands. The bouncing body is always ready to clamber up the nearest tree, engage in a mock battle with his brothers, or splash in the nearest mud puddle.

The woodland clown

If the racoon can be called playful, its large cousin, the bear, can be called a clown. Few animals seem to get into more scrapes – and out of them again – than a bear. Starting from the time it is a cub, a bear investigates almost anything it can get one paw into.

Bears like to eat honey. They also like the grubs that are found in hornet nests. Their fur is so thick that the peppery insects can seldom sting them. The nose of a bear is tender, however. It may sit whimpering in the middle of an angry swarm of bees, swatting and rubbing them off its nose, but getting stickier by the minute.

Sometimes the wires on a telephone pole start humming in the wind. The sound seems to a bear like the sound of a hive of bees. It may pull the pole to pieces with its great claws, looking for the insects that are not there. At other times it will sit soberly and watch the marching of a stream of ants. Then it may turn and thrash the life out of a nearby bush.

Since bears may visit rubbish dumps in wild areas, the cubs often get their heads caught in tin cans. Then they run backwards all over the dump, trying to get away. Their wails are answered by the growl of the mother. Added to it all is the clatter and racket of all the rubbish as the cub frantically tries to escape.

Bear cubs are hardy little creatures. They have to be, for their mother may tumble them head over heels if they do not obey her. One bear cub was seen getting slapped by its mother, while the cub's brother seemed to be almost laughing at the punishment. The first cub just waited his chance. When his mother was not looking he knocked his brother flat.

Through all their bumps and scrapes, bears keep up their playful spirit. No wonder they are called the clowns of the woods.

Homo sapiens – the funniest animal of all

Many people think monkeys are the funniest animals. They run and steal things and play tricks on each other. They love to poke other monkeys when they are sleeping or even drop things on them when they are not looking. But when you visit a zoo, you can usually see an even funnier animal. This is the creature just outside the bars making faces and funny noises and sticking its fingers in its ears to get the monkey to imitate it.

This creature, of course, is man. Even while there may be wars, poverty and sickness, people keep their sense of humour. This is one of the best things about Homo sapiens – the human race. Our sense of humour helps us get along even in the hardest of conditions. This is lucky, for man is probably the only animal that worries. The rest of the animals just take each day as it comes.

There are many creatures that are natural comedians. With your own sense of humour and a little time, you can find them for yourself – and have fun doing it.

But, remember – do not laugh too hard at the other animals. Think how we must look to them!

INDEX

Picture Credits